PRACTICAL
CRITICAL THINKING

for Grades 9-12+
Teacher's Manual

Written by
Catherine Connors-Nelson

Graphic Design by
Chip Dombrowski

© 2015
THE CRITICAL THINKING CO.™
www.CriticalThinking.com
Phone: 800-458-4849 • Fax: 541-756-1758
1991 Sherman Ave., Suite 200 • North Bend • OR 97459
ISBN 978-1-60144-770-8

MIX
Paper from
responsible sources
FSC® C011935

Table of Contents

Part I: Answers

Unit 1: Becoming a Critical Thinker
Chapter 1..1-5
Chapter 2..6-8

Unit 2: Adding to My Critical Thinking Toolbox
Chapter 3..9-18
Chapter 4..19-28

Unit 3: Critical Thinking and Arguments
Chapter 5..29-39
Chapter 6..40-46

Unit 4: Applying My Critical Thinking
Chapter 7..47-59
Chapter 8..60-68

Part II: Reproducible Activities

List of Activities ....Rii
Chapter 1..R1-R15
Chapter 2..R16-R33
Chapter 3..R34-R53
Chapter 4..R54-R78
Chapter 5..R79-R120
Chapter 6..R121-R154
Chapter 7..R155-R200
Chapter 8..R201-R228

Part I
Answers

Chapter 1
The 411 About Critical Thinking

1.1   (pages 1-3)

A World Without Critical Thinking Thought Experiment (p. 1): Answers will vary. Students need to demonstrate that they've thought about what life would actually be like if no one engaged in critical thinking and how they would be personally impacted. The point of this activity is for them to identify for themselves the value of critical thinking and the role it plays in their lives. This requires them to use many of the cognitive skills important to critical thinking: comprehension, analysis, evaluation, and communication.

My Prediction (p. 3): Predictions will vary. The students need to think about the cartoon "The Anatomy of the Teen Brain" and predict what it has to do with the chapter. They will have an opportunity to revise their predictions during the chapter. The application of neuroscience research to learning shows the value of predictions for helping students buy into learning about a topic. It also requires them to use the cognitive skills of analysis and evaluation. This prediction activity is getting students to think about how their brain and the size of the various centers in the brain relate to critical thinking. The tie-in is that the brain of the teenager and young adult is still developing, especially the prefrontal cortex (the CEO of the brain) and that affects their ability to engage in critical thinking. Their executive functions of reasoning, judgment, planning, and impulse control are limited and will continue to develop until their mid-twenties (around 26 years old). So one of the obstacles to critical thinking for teens and young adults is that their brain is still developing and being restructured.

1.2   (pages 4-5)

Critical Thinking Skills Quiz   (p. 4)

Creativity	Comprehension
Analysis	Evaluation
Construction	Communication

Activity Thought Experiment (p. 4): Answers will vary. Students are to evaluate an activity they like to do in terms of how well they did it the first time and the role practice plays in learning the activity and getting better at it. This is to help them buy into practicing their critical thinking skills.

Prediction Revision (p. 5): Students have an opportunity to revise their predictions based on what they have learned already. They may choose not to revise their prediction. This is another way of reinforcing buy-in and interest.

"What Is Critical Thinking?" Thought Experiment (p. 5): Designs will vary. In this Thought Experiment, students need to explain what critical thinking is and why it is important. By designing their own webpage, they will use many of their critical thinking skills as well as reinforce what they've learned about critical thinking as they select the content to put on their webpage. If there is time in class, have the students share their webpages with one another in small groups. If you have a website for your class, consider having the class select one of these to use. You may choose to have students continue to contribute to the class website for each chapter. This will enable them to teach one another and can be used as a coaching tool for students who need it or would like to refresh their learning.

1.3   (page 6)

Student Poll (p. 6): Answers will vary. Students are to read the story and rate the level of critical thinking going on in the story. This enables them to use several critical thinking skills, such as comprehension and evaluation, and see the real-life application of critical thinking (or the lack of it!).

1.4   (pages 7-17)

Student Poll (p. 8): Answers will vary. This poll focuses on what the students learned about the relationship between their ability to reason and engage in critical thinking and the development of their brains. The poll has them apply what they are learning to themselves.

"I Could Have Done Better" Thought Experiment (p. 8): Answers will vary. Students are to examine their own lives in terms of a time when they could have done a better job using critical thinking and then to analyze what might have been an obstacle for them in using their critical thinking. It is important that students connect what they are learning with their lives—this is what makes learning about critical thinking worthwhile and meaningful. This also facilitates greater buy-in and interest to learn more about the obstacles to critical thinking.

Egocentrism Obstacle (p. 9): Answers will vary. Student answers need to demonstrate that they comprehend the topic of egocentrism, are able to analyze it, and make the connection themselves (before they read about it) about why egocentrism would be an obstacle to critical thinking.

Egocentrism Thought Experiment (p. 9): Answers will vary. Student answers need to demonstrate that they comprehend what egocentrism is and how it is an obstacle to critical thinking. Then they need to be able to take it a step further and figure out how they would overcome this obstacle. Possible answers focus on: (1) explaining to the friend that everyone has to work on his or her critical thinking, that it is possible to overcome this obstacle, and that the first step is recognizing that he has a problem with this obstacle, (2) helping the friend identify how and when he engages in self-interested thinking or self-serving bias, (3) helping the friend by looking at a specific incident when egocentrism was an obstacle to critical thinking—doing this by helping the friend identify how he acted like an egoist in his thinking and then by brainstorming with this friend about how he could have used his critical thinking by looking at the big picture and getting a realistic view of the event and how it affected other people.

Student Poll (p. 10): Answers will vary. This poll has students apply the concept of peer pressure to their own lives, and it demonstrates to them the positive impact it can have in their lives.

Peer Pressure Thought Experiment (p. 11): Answers will vary. This activity requires students to demonstrate that they comprehend what peer pressure is and how it can be an obstacle to critical thinking. It also requires them to use the critical thinking skills of construction and creativity as they create the four tips and a slogan or some graphic ideas. Some possible tips are:

- Believe in yourself and stand up for your values.
- Be an independent thinker.
- Remember, it's okay to say "no" to your friends when they want to do something that you know isn't right.
- Stay away from kids who pressure you to do things you don't think are right to do.

- Have a friend who will say "no" too.
- Talk to someone you trust if you are having problems with peer pressure.

Assumption Thought Experiment (p. 12): Answers will vary. Students need to demonstrate that they understand what an assumption is, that they can recognize when they've made an assumption, and that they realize how it affects their lives.

Student Poll (p. 13): Answers will vary. This poll reveals how well students understand unreasonable assumptions and the application to their lives. If anyone put a score above 5, then the student either does not understand the concept or does not want to admit to making unreasonable assumptions. If you find that many students have numbers like this, then you need to spend some time exploring further what an unreasonable assumption is and look at some examples—particularly of stereotypes.

Emotion and Critical Thinking Practice I (p. 14): Answers will vary. Student answers need to demonstrate that they are trying to analyze and evaluate if and how emotion might be an obstacle to critical thinking. The two men are very angry and fighting verbally. Their critical thinking will be hurt by the emotion they are feeling, especially the level of the emotion. While angry people can process information logically and rationally, these two men have had their critical thinking hurt because they have lost control and given in to their anger, forgetting to use their critical thinking skills. Evidence of this is all over the floor around them!

Emotion and Critical Thinking Practice II (p. 15): Answers will vary. Student answers need to demonstrate that they are trying to analyze and evaluate if and how emotion might be an obstacle to critical thinking. The teenage girl is crying and looks very upset. Her critical thinking will more than likely be hurt. Her processing of information will focus on detail and not on what she already knows. This happens because of how her affect impacts her recall. Her negative affect may also cause her to make pessimistic judgments and affect the evaluation of her options by overestimating negative outcomes and underestimating positive ones.

Student Poll (p. 16): Answers will vary. This poll provides students with a fun way to evaluate their own experience with the critical thinking obstacles in this section. This poll will be the basis of another activity in section 1.6.

1.5   (pages 18-19)

Important Takeaways (p. 19): The point of this activity is application. Students are to evaluate the content of the chapter and decide what three things they want to remember and use in their own lives. These takeaways are not concerned with what is important to remember for a test.

1.6   (pages 20-22)

1. **The Best Critical Thinkers I Know** (p. 20): Answers will vary. Students need to identify the best critical thinkers they know. They can select people from their own lives or people from the news who they think are good critical thinkers. Students need to be able to explain why these people are good critical thinkers. This will require them to analyze and evaluate what makes these people good critical thinkers and then abstract the characteristics of a good critical thinker so that they can write a description.

2. **Insanity and Albert Einstein** (p. 21): To do something over and over again that does not work shows a lack of critical thinking. Good critical thinking would mean recognizing that what you are doing does not work, understanding why it does not work, coming up with alternative solutions, and then trying one of them out.

3. **Pumping Up** (p. 21): The picture of the brain pumping iron reminds us that we need to practice our critical thinking skills—that our ability as critical thinkers grows in proportion to our use of these skills. The more we use these skills, the better we are at critical thinking.

4. **My Top Two Obstacles to Critical Thinking** (p. 22): Answers will vary. Students need to rank the list of critical thinking obstacles according to their experience. This requires them to understand why these are obstacles to critical thinking and evaluate how these obstacles relate to their own lives. Students must identify which two obstacles happen to them the most. They also need to be able to think of ways that they can make the obstacles they've selected less potent in their lives. Activity 6 in the Group Activities follows up on this by having the students coach each other on ways to deal with the obstacles that are the biggest problems for their critical thinking and by having the class discuss ideas for dealing with them.

1.7   (pages 23-24)

1. **A World Without Critical Thinking** (p. 23): Answers will vary. This activity follows up on the *A World Without Critical Thinking Thought Experiment* in Section 1.1 that asks what the world would be like without critical thinking, especially in their own lives. Working in small groups will encourage more discussion from all the members of the group. Circulate around the room, helping the students personalize this question and see the value and importance of critical thinking. Concretizing will be particularly helpful.

2. **The Best Critical Thinkers I Know** (p. 23): Answers will vary. This activity is a continuation of Individual Activity #1. By working in pairs, students can collaborate on a new description of critical thinking based on their answers. This allows them to coach one another; evaluate again what belongs in a description of critical thinking; use their critical thinking skills in tandem with another person, which is important because they need to learn how to be an independent thinker when working with others; and communicate what they think makes a good critical thinker. As a class, the group will discuss the list of attributes created by all the pairs, evaluate them, and decide on the top five attributes. This activity hones their understanding of what characteristics or attributes make up a critical thinker as well as gets them to use their critical thinking skills.

3. **Patient Files** (p. 23): Answers will vary. This activity enables students to verbalize how they rated the critical thinking going on in the story as well as their rationale for the rating, to consider and discuss any different perspectives other students may have about the critical thinking in the story, and to work as a class to identify alternative solutions that the hospital could have used to solve its problem.

4. **You and Your Brain** (p. 23): The clue in the cartoon was how small the "Reasoning and Good Judgment Gland" was compared to the size of the other areas of the brain. The students' brain development relates to critical thinking because their brains are still developing and being restructured. This means that preteens, teens, and young adults will have deficits in critical thinking, particularly since the prefrontal cortex is still developing (the part of the brain that is the "CEO" and responsible for reasoning, judgment, planning, and impulse control), they are more plugged into the limbic area

of the brain (an area especially connected to emotions), and because the speed of communication between the brain cells (neurons) does not have the speed of adult brains (myelination—the insulation on the fibers, or axons, that connect the neurons and facilitates the speed of communication between the neurons—is not yet complete). However, students can positively impact the development of their brains, especially the areas in the brain associated with critical thinking skills. This occurs when they practice and use their critical thinking skills. Allow them to discuss their reaction to what they learned about their brain development and how they might have drawn the cartoon.

5. **I Could Have Done Better** (p. 24): Answers will vary. This activity is based on the "I Could Have Done Better" Thought Experiment in 1.4. Have a volunteer share a time when he or she needed to use critical thinking and could have done a better job using it. Have the students analyze this story so that they can identify the obstacle(s) to critical thinking. Then have them discuss what the student could have done differently and which of the critical thinking skills needed to be used. This discussion will reinforce what the students have learned; enable them to apply what they've learned, particularly as they construct solutions; and enable them to experience how they are able to help one of their peers improve his or her critical thinking through coaching.

6. **My Top Two Obstacles to Critical Thinking** (p. 24): Answers will vary. This activity follows up on Individual Activity #4 by having students work in pairs to coach each other on ways to deal with the obstacles that are the biggest problems for their critical thinking. Coaching reinforces the learning while personalizing its application. In addition, the class reveal of the individual rankings of the obstacles shows the students that everyone has obstacles and that other students may face the same ones that they do. The large group discussion about how to deal with the obstacles will provide other options and suggestions for the students to consider when dealing with these obstacles.

7. **Tips for Dealing with Peer Pressure** (p. 24): Answers will vary. This is an important activity because of the immense power that peer pressure has on critical thinking, especially for preteens, teenagers, and young adults. This activity follows up on the *Peer Pressure Thought Experiment* in section 1.4. Have the students discuss their tips for dealing with peer pressure and brainstorm additional ideas. Select a student to be the recorder and put the tips on the board so that everyone can see them. If you have additional ideas that you feel need to be listed, then add them when the students have exhausted their ideas. Have the students select the top 5 tips and have them discuss a way to share these tips with other students in the school. Perhaps even select the best slogan and graphic idea to go with the top 5 tips. Sharing this information as a class with the school takes their learning from the theoretical to real-life application. It enables them to see that what they are learning in this book has meaning and application in their personal lives and in society.

Chapter 2
Playing Games, Doing Puzzles: Practicing Critical Thinking Skills

2.1   (pages 25-26)

My Brain Tattoo (p. 26): Designs will vary. The brain tattoos that students create need to convey the message: "Our ability as critical thinkers grows in proportion to our use of our critical thinking skills. The more we use them, the better we are at critical thinking." Allow them the freedom to design their brain tattoo. They can use symbols or images along with words to convey the message. Implicit learning and reinforcement of the message will occur as they wrestle with their design.

2.2   (pages 27-29)

Footprints (p. 27)

1. F; 6, picture; caption; The footprints lead toward the water.

2. T; 5, 6, 7; Sentences 5, 6, and 7 tell us that when Ted woke up, he could not find his brother. George wasn't lying on his towel, which was still on the sand, and George's car keys and car were still there. Because of this, he didn't know where his brother was.

3. U; There is not enough evidence. Since both Ted and George love to go swimming at the beach, it is probable that they did go swimming together, though we cannot know this with certainty.

4. T; 3, 5, 6, 7, 8, picture, caption; Sentence 3 suggests that George loves to swim at the beach, and sentences 5 and 7 indicate that George's car keys and towel are still there, and the car is still in the parking lot. Plus we know from sentence 8 that George would never leave Ted alone at the beach with no way home. Sentence 6, the caption, and the picture tell us that Ted does not see anyone on the beach, but he does see footprints leading into the water. Based on all of this evidence, Ted's conclusion that George has gone swimming is most likely true.

5. F; There is no certain evidence that the footprints must belong to George. While the footprints probably belong to George, they may also belong to someone else who might be swimming. We are not told anything about how many people are or are not swimming in the water.

Surfing (pp. 28-29)

1. a; 5; Females can be great surfers, surfing professionally. Stephanie Gilmore is an example of this as the 2012 Women's Professional World champion.

2. e; There is not enough evidence. We don't know who else in Charlie's family surfs besides her mom.

3. c; 7, 9; Surfing involves skills just like other sports do. In order to be good, a surfer must practice those skills.

4. e; There is not enough evidence. While Charlie's mom taught her to surf, we do not know how talented a surfer her mom was or is. Charlie's talent for surfing may be unique in her family.

5. d; 4, 5, 7; Sentence 4 tells us that Charlie places 1st in many amateur surfing competitions. Sentence 5 says she wants to be one of the top professional surfers someday. Sentence 7 explains that it takes a lot of strength and endurance to surf, especially on the professional level. Given Charlie's drive to win and become a top professional surfer, it is probably false that she never does any type of strength or

endurance training. This is particularly true since professional surfers, like other professional athletes, do physical training, working on core strength, balance, and endurance. Professional surfers like Stephanie Gilmore, who Charlie wants to emulate, are an example of this. It would be unlikely that Charlie is not aware of the physical training, including strength and endurance training, that Stephanie Gilmore engages in.

6. c; 9; picture, caption; Turning on a wave, or carving, is not the same thing as cutting back. The photo shows Charlie turning on a wave, or carving, and the caption indicates that she is starting to carve.

2.3 (page 30)

Quotation (p. 30)

Wisdom is better than rubies, and all the things that may be desired are not to be compared to it.

Squares (p. 30)

30. There are 16 1×1 squares, nine 2×2 squares, four 3×3 squares and one 4×4 square.

2.4 (Page 31)

Seven Chairs (p. 31)

A mother has two daughters, who each have two daughters. So each of the three mothers has two daughters, which makes six women, plus we need to count the matriarch, which brings the total to 7. So the seven chairs are sufficient for seating all the women.

2.5 (Pages 32-35)

Dr. Funster's Visual Mind Benders® (pp. 34-35)

1.

2.

2.6 (Pages 36-41)

Class President (p. 38)

STUDENT	CANDIDATE
Agnes	Grant
Betsy	Sterling
Cornelius	McGuire
Dexter	Houh

A boy voted for McGuire (1), but he isn't Dexter (1), so he is Cornelius. Betsy didn't vote for Houh or Grant (2), so she voted for Sterling. Agnes didn't vote for Houh (3), so Dexter did, and Agnes voted for Grant.

Part-time Jobs (p. 39)

NAME	JOB	CELL PHONE COLOR
Jeanette	paper route	green
Marcia	carpenter's apprentice	red
Saralee	cook	blue
Theodora	delivery person	white

Two of the girls live on one street, and the other two live on another street (1). One of these pairs of girls are the carpenter's apprentice and the person with the white cell phone (1). Jeanette and the cook are also one of these pairs (2), but they are not the same pair, since the cook neither has the white cell phone (4) nor is the carpenter's apprentice. Then Jeanette and the cook are the other pair in clue 1—that is, they are Saralee and the person with the green cell phone. Jeanette isn't Saralee, so she has the green cell phone, and so Saralee is the cook. Then the carpenter's apprentice and the person with the white cell phone (1) are also Marcia and the delivery person (2). The carpenter's apprentice isn't the delivery person, so she is Marcia. Then the delivery person has the white cell phone. The delivery person is not Jeanette (green cell phone), Marcia (2), or Saralee (cook), so she is Theodora. Then Marcia, who lives on the same street as Theodora (2), has the red cell phone (3). This leaves Saralee with the blue cell phone and Jeanette with the paper route.

Pet Cats (pp. 40-41)

NAME	COLOR	CAT
Abner Magland	yellow	Pretty
Crystal Harmon	black	Kitty
Edmund Dinton	white	Sleepy
Joy Landon	gray	Fluffy

Magland has the yellow cat (1). Crystal doesn't have the yellow cat (5), so she is not Magland. Also, she isn't Landon or Dinton (3), so she is Harmon. Abner isn't Landon or Dinton (3), so he is Magland. Two of the cats are short-haired, and the other two are long-haired (3), so Edmund owns a long-haired cat (4). Then he is Dinton (3), and so Joy is Landon. Abner Magland's yellow cat is short-haired (3), so it is Pretty (4). Then Landon owns the gray cat (3, 4). Crystal doesn't have the white cat, so Edmund has it, and Crystal's cat is black. Sleepy is not owned by Joy or Crystal Harmon (2), so Sleepy is Edmund's cat. Crystal doesn't own Fluffy (5), so she owns Kitty, and Joy owns Fluffy.

2.7 (pages 42-43)

Takeaways (p. 43): The students need to identify three takeaways from the chapter. This requires them to evaluate how they used their critical thinking skills and what they learned in the process. These takeaways need to focus on what they feel is important for them to personally remember. The focus is not on what they think they need to remember for a test.

Chapter 3
Some Basic Concepts for Critical Thinking

3.1   (page 44)

Toolbox Thought Experiment (p. 44): Answers will vary. The students need to demonstrate that they have made the connection between critical thinking and their own lives by identifying what tools they need to add to their critical thinking toolbox to help them become better critical thinkers. The names of these tools are not particularly important. What is important is that they can describe the tools and explain how they would help them with their critical thinking. Some examples of what students might say are:

- The Good Argument Evaluator—a tool to help me evaluate arguments so that I know which ones are good and to accept.
- The Scam Sniffer—a tool to help me sniff out scams in advertising.
- The Evidence Tool—a tool to help me decide when to accept evidence or not as trustworthy.

3.2   (pages 45-50)

Student Poll (p. 45): Answers will vary. This poll has students identify where they encounter facts and opinions. It also has them explain what they think a fact is and what they think an opinion is before the section provides definitions for these terms. This will help their buy-in. There is no "wrong" answer in the sense that this is based on the students' experience; both facts and opinions can be found in all of the listed locations. In 3.7 Group Activities & Discussion activity #1, the class will discuss their answers to this student poll and any differences they might have.

Definitions of Fact & Opinion (p. 45): Answers will vary. Students are to define both of these words. This facilitates their thought around the difference between the meanings of the two words. Engaging in some initial thought about a topic will help them buy into what they are learning.

My Prediction (p. 46): Predictions will vary. Students are to make a prediction about the connection between the picture of the woman knitting the hat and the chapter topic, which centers around examining some basic concepts in critical thinking that are important to add to their toolbox. Specifically, this prediction relates to creativity and creative problem solving and the importance of these for critical thinking. Creativity is an important cognitive skill for critical thinkers, and it is particularly important in problem solving. When creative thinking is applied to a problem, critical thinkers make use of their factual knowledge, skills, and special talents; their ability to come up with lots of new solutions to a problem (divergent thinking); and their ability then to make the best choice among all possible solutions (convergent thinking). Creativity and creative problem solving also make use of many other interacting cognitive processes and emotions in the brain.

Example of an Opinion Using a Signal Word (p. 47): Answers will vary. The student is to create their own example of an opinion using a signal word. The activity will reinforce the learning about signal words for opinions. Consider using the student examples in class as you discuss this topic.

Student Poll (p. 48): This poll allows students to struggle with the difference between a fact and an opinion. The example is an opinion because it represents what the friend thinks or believes—in this case, the friend believes that what Dr. George said actually proves that most patients would opt for less aggressive treatment for back pain if they were informed about all the risks and benefits of all the treatments. While Dr. George may have stated that most patients would choose less aggressive treatment for back pain, no evidence was provided by the friend that proves what the patients would do or even that what he says has any bearing on the matter at all. We might want to know: Who is Dr. Sam George? What is his expertise? Is he qualified to speak about this topic, i.e., is he an authority on back pain?

Fact or Opinion? Practice (p. 50): Remember, the issue is whether these are facts or opinions and not whether the facts are true or not.

1. Fact. This statistic can be verified as to whether or not it is true or false. One place to look would be the website of the Bureau of Labor Statistics, part of the U.S. Department of Labor.

2. Opinion. This statement reflects someone's beliefs about Mayor Marks. No evidence is provided to prove that Mayor Marks does not know how to solve the housing shortage in the city.

3. Fact. The credit card company Visa conducted a survey of 2,000 people in 2012 regarding the economic impact on how much the Tooth Fairy leaves. The amount paid out per tooth increased 15% in 2012 over 2011. Visa's senior director of global financial education said that it is due to "a combination of things: one is a reflection of an improving economy and that parents feel they can afford to be generous in small areas. The other driver is parental angst. It is very hard for us to say 'no' to our kids." Additional larger studies could be done to further verify the veracity of the findings of this study or to challenge the results.

4. Fact. This can be proven true or false. It is true that some grade schools now provide iPads for use in the classroom. A quick Google search provides examples of this, such as at Downers Grove Grade School District 58 in Illinois, the Virginia Department of Education pilot program, the Concord School District in New Hampshire, and at South Mountain Elementary School in Millburn, New Jersey.

5. Opinion. This comment reflects someone's belief that because of the record amount of profit made by U.S. auto manufacturers, there is no reason for the U.S. auto industry to be complaining. No evidence is provided to prove that this is true that they are actually making record profits. A clue that this is an opinion is the language that is used: "I don't feel sorry for the auto industry," "having it great right now" and "making fistfuls of dollars." It may actually be a fact that the U.S. auto manufacturers have made the highest amount of profit today than ever before. This could be verified one way or another. However, we are presented with an opinion that is dressed up to look like a fact.

Student Poll (p. 50): Answers will vary. Students are asked to evaluate the critical thinking of the mother in the true story from *Reader's Digest*. This helps students see that what they are learning has real-life application and it reinforces their learning about critical thinking.

3.3   (pages 51-53)

Star Trek Thought Experiment (p. 51): Answers will vary. Students need to articulate their position regarding whether or not there are aliens living on other planets. They will then be able to reflect on this position in terms of whether they believe that it is possible, probable, or proven that alien life exists. This will enable buy-in and help them apply the concepts of the lesson to their own position.

Prediction Revision (p. 51): Now that students have experienced predictions in chapter 1, they know what to expect. The opportunity for revision will encourage them to reflect on what they have learned already and do some creative thinking and creative problem solving—which is what the picture will introduce.

Possible? Probable? Proven? Practice (p. 53)

1. Possible. Bigfoot is described as a primate, approximately 8 feet tall, and a cross between a gorilla and a human. There have been witnesses and stories of Bigfoot originating from Native American folklore before Europeans arrived in North America until today. It is biologically possible that a very large primate exists in the United States. We do not have enough evidence to cross the threshold of probable, even though there are many eyewitnesses. There is some scientific evidence collected by Dr. Grover Krantz from Washington State University. In the 1960s he examined photos and casts of footprints from across Washington that appeared to have been made by very large primates walking upright. At least one set seemed very convincing, although there is the possibility that it was created by an artist "with expert understanding of primate foot anatomy" (http://animal.discovery.com). There is also film (The Patterson-Gimlin film) of Bigfoot, or sasquatches, taken in 1967 in northern California. This evidence only points to the possibility that such creatures exist.

2. None. There is no evidence at this time that aquatic humanoids exist or have ever been found despite the legends. The National Ocean and Atmospheric Administration in 2013 released a statement that says: "The belief in mermaids may have arisen at the very dawn of our species, but are mermaids real? No evidence of aquatic humanoids has ever been found. Why, then, do they occupy the collective unconscious of nearly all seafaring peoples? That's a question best left to historians, philosophers, and anthropologists."

3. Proven. NASA scientists, in September 2013, released the first-ever recording of sounds in interstellar space. These sounds were recorded by Voyager 1 in 2012 after it left our solar system. As explained on PBS (www.pbs.org): "The plasma in the heliosphere (a bullet-shaped bubble that surrounds the sun which Voyager 1 had to pass through to get to interstellar space) and in interstellar space have different densities. When solar flares send ripples through the plasma, causing the particles to vibrate, two antennae on Voyager pick up the frequency and transmit it back to Earth as an audible radio transmission."

4. Proven. *Issus coleoptratus*, a species of plant-hopping insect, is the first known insect that has interlocking gears that actually work on its hind legs. This was discovered by Dr. Malcolm Burrows and Dr. Gregory Sutton and captured on a video. Dr. Burrows is Emeritus Professor of Neurobiology (Department of Zoology) at the University of Cambridge in the United Kingdom, and Dr. Sutton is a researcher at the University of Bristol.

5. Proven. Butterflies in the western Amazon rainforest drink the tears of turtles because the tears contain sodium that is found in the salt in the tears. Sodium is a necessary mineral for butterflies and not easily found by them in the Amazon. Butterflies feeding on turtle tears is a common sight in the Amazon, so common that it easier to photograph this occurring than to photograph the turtles without them.

3.4   (pages 54-58)

Did Beth Notsofast steal the wallet and the money? (p. 54): Answers will vary. Students are asked to make a judgment as to whether or not Beth Notsofast stole the wallet and money. They must cite their evidence for their "Yes" or "No" answer, and if they feel the answer is "unknown", then they must explain this answer and their evaluation that there is a lack of evidence. This exercise provides students with an introductory experience evaluating evidence.

Case of the Missing Wallet (pp. 56-57)

Judy's conclusion: Sentence 16: "Beth Notsofast stole my wallet and all the money for my new track uniform."

Evidence #1: No. While Beth's presence in the locker room does not prove that she stole the wallet, it does open up the possibility that she could have stolen the wallet and money. However, someone else may have stolen the wallet before she entered the locker room. We have no idea exactly when the theft occurred. Beth's presence also raises suspicion because she doesn't belong in the locker room at that time because she is not on the track team. We see in sentence 2 that Judy is surprised to see Beth there.

Evidence #2: No. We do not know when the theft occurred. Beth may have entered the locker room after the theft occurred. We do not even know if Beth saw that Judy's locker was open or that she knows which locker belongs to Judy, nor do we know if she was even aware that Judy brought money to school to pay for her uniform. If Beth does know which locker is Judy's, then it is suspicious that when she sees Judy she says nothing about her open locker.

Evidence #3: No; but as sentence 3 points out, it is unusual that Beth doesn't greet Judy or even look her in the eye since they are "really good" friends. Judy is puzzled by Beth's behavior; in fact, Beth's behavior might suggest that she is ashamed or embarrassed about something that involves her and Judy, and it creates suspicion about what she might have been up to in the locker room or even what she might know about the theft.

Evidence #4: No; it only proves that someone broke into her locker.

Score: Overall, the evidence is definitely not conclusive. However, the fact that Beth was in the locker room at a time when she doesn't belong there, that she is obviously uncomfortable looking Judy in the eye or greeting her when they are good friends, and that she comes out of the empty locker room does raise the possibility that she might have stolen the wallet and money. Yet, there is not enough evidence to even move it to being probable that she committed the theft.

If students feel certain that Beth stole the wallet, then they need to consider what type of evidence might shake that certainty; for example, what if she did have a reason to be in the locker room at that time: e.g., to get something out of her locker that she forgot earlier or if she was there looking for someone. Other evidence might be that she wasn't in the locker room long enough to commit the theft.

If students don't feel certain that Beth stole the wallet, then they need to consider what type of evidence they would need in order to be convinced—evidence such as Beth's fingerprints on the door handle of Judy's locker or Judy's wallet in Beth's purse.

Check-in (p. 58): In this check-in students will assess how well they understand the evaluation of evidence and what it would take to make their confidence a 10. It is also geared to teach the students that they are partners in their education with their teacher and the other students in their class. Teachers are advised to follow up on the poll results and encourage students who need help to get some coaching either from them or from one of the other students.

The Evidence in Arguments Quiz (p. 58)

1. evidence
2. supports
3. true; false
4. true
5. kind of evidence   accuracy of evidence
   relevancy of evidence   quality of evidence
   quantity of evidence

3.5   (pages 59-66)

Student Poll (p. 59): Answers will vary. Students are asked to evaluate the woman's creative problem solving. This begins to prime them regarding the upcoming discussion on the use of creativity, creative thinking, and creative problem solving. This poll also helps students buy into the lesson.

If You Needed to Knit a Hat (p. 60): Answers will vary. Students need to analyze the problem of knitting a hat and identify some of the things they would need to consider in order to do this. This has them apply their critical thinking skills to a new situation (since most students probably have never knitted a hat). Once they answer the question, they are provided with immediate feedback in terms of things to consider.

My Creative Problem Solving Thought Experiment (p. 60): Answers will vary. Students analyze how they used creative problem solving in the past. They need to be as specific and concrete as possible. This activity is the basis of activity #7 in 3.8 Group Activities & Discussion.

The Incomplete Figure (p. 61): Drawings will vary. This activity is similar to the ones found in the Torrance Test of Creative Thinking. It engages the students in creative thinking in a fun way. In doing this activity, students are forced to see beyond what is presented and be innovative. This type of figure allows them to engage in creativity without being paralyzed by being "right."

Nine Dot Thought Experiment (p. 62):

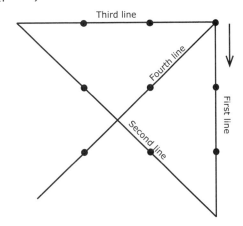

"Aha!" Thought Experiment (p. 63): Answers will vary. Students are to describe a time when they had sudden insight or inspiration. Sudden inspiration occurs in creative thinking and creative problem solving; however, most of the time creative thinking involves trial and error as we test our ideas, which often leads to further innovation.

Inspiration Thought Experiment (p. 63): Answers will vary. This activity has students identify their own triggers for inspiration and then evaluate which are the top three triggers. This makes students aware of the behaviors that often facilitate their creative thinking and also introduces them to other possible aids. Having the class share their top three triggers for inspiration would allow the students to see what they have in common and how they might be different and why.

Check-in (p. 66): Encourage the students who have selected the dog sleeping on the laptop to seek coaching so that they can gain confidence in understanding the information in the chapter.

3.6   (pages 67-69)

Important Takeaways (p. 69): The students need to think about what they learned in this chapter and identify three takeaways that are important to them for their life. This activity makes the content of the chapter personally relevant to them.

3.7   (pages 70-71)

1. **Incomplete Figure** (p. 70): Drawings will vary. The students have the opportunity to engage in further creative thought.

2. **Divide the Figure** (p. 70):

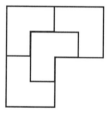

3. **The Candle Problem** (p. 71): Dump the thumbtacks out of the box. Push the thumbtacks through the cardboard box into the wall. Light the candle and use drops of wax to secure the candle upright in the box.

4. **The Case of the Lead Masks** (p. 71): See problem #7 in 3.8 Group Activities & Discussion Activity.

3.8   (pages 72-79)

1. **Fact or Opinion?** (p. 72): Answers will vary. This activity follows up on the *Fact or Opinion? Practice* in section 3.2. It is important to encourage discussion between the students. This allows them to practice the critical thinking skill of communication. Make sure the students understand the difference between a fact and an opinion and why it matters. The "Why" is always important for buy-in.

2. **Aliens** (p. 72): Answers will vary. Working in small groups will encourage all of the students to participate in discussing their answers to the *Star Trek Thought Experiment* in Section 3.3. Encourage them to coach one another on the distinction between possible, probable, and proven as well as why the distinction is important.

3. **Possible? Probable? Proven?** (p. 72): Answers will vary. This activity should be a catalyst for some lively and interesting discussion. Requiring each group to come up with one solution that they all agree on will encourage this discussion, though you may need to circulate so that no student dominates his or her small group discussion. The discussion as a class and the need to arrive at one answer will also facilitate discussion and coaching by the students for others in the class. Make sure that by the end of the class session students understand the difference between possible, probable, and proven. They should also be able to articulate why the distinction is important as a critical thinker. See section 3.3 answers to *Possible? Probable? Proven? Practice.*

4. **The Case of the Missing Wallet** (p. 73): Working in pairs will facilitate coaching between the students on how to evaluate evidence. Having their evaluations summarized on the board will show the students how others evaluated the evidence, and the class discussion will either reinforce their learning about how to evaluate evidence or help them learn where they made a mistake in their evaluation of the evidence and how to do an even better job next time. The case study approach is one that facilitates discussion and buy-in.

5. **The Candle Problem** (p. 73): See the solution in 3.7 answers #3 The Candle Problem.

6. **My Creative Problem Solving** (p. 73): Answers will vary, but each student needs to share their answers to the My Creative Problem Solving Thought Experiment in 3.5. Every student should come up with an example of a problem they needed to solve, how they found the solution to the problem, and what the solution was. Their answers should be specific and concrete—not vague.

7. **The Case of the Lead Masks** (pp. 73-79): This activity uses the case study approach to look at a real-life case that was never solved. Having the students work in pairs will encourage all of the students to participate in the activity and prepare them to participate in the class discussion.

A. **Evaluating the Evidence** (pp. 76-78)

1. PT; The suits (sentence 2) suggest that the men were probably meeting someone; however, it is not conclusive given that we do not know their usual attire. We also have the eyewitness report (sentence 18) that Viana was very nervous and checked his watch frequently. When this is coupled with the note which says "be at the agreed place" at 4:30 p.m., there becomes circumstantial evidence that that the men were probably meeting someone.

2. PT; Sentence 5 tells us that each man was found at the site wearing a lead mask—the kind that protects people against radiation, meaning a solid mask with no eye holes (see the photos of the masks) and made of material to provide protection. It was important enough to them to have protection that they constructed the masks in Viana's workshop (6). We also have the note that says in sentence 11 that after they swallowed the capsules and the capsules took effect, they were to "protect metals" and "wait for the mask signal." While we do not know what kind of metals the note refers to, whether they had the metals with them or expected to receive them, or even what the "mask signal" refers to, it is probably true that the two men expected to encounter some form of radiation, which probably was connected to the metals.

3. U; There is no evidence in the case study that da Cruz and Viana were conducting an experiment at the time. While it is a possibility, the lack of any evidence will not allow us to claim that this statement is probably true.

4. False; Sentence 3 tells us there were no signs of violence on the bodies of either man and no signs of trauma or of a struggle in the area around the bodies. The coroner's report (sentence 25) confirms this by establishing that there were no injuries on the bodies. So the evidence leads us to conclude that this statement is false.

5. PF; While sentence 23 tells us that the money for the car disappeared, we have no evidence as to what happened to it. In fact, there is no direct evidence that the men had taken enough money to buy a car, though it was reported that they had taken enough money to buy a car. Reports about this case do not indicate how the person who reported this knew that they had taken enough money to buy a car. Did the person see the money? Did the person not see the money, but instead was told by the men that they had the money? The lack of a struggle around the bodies and the lack of injuries on the bodies make murder during a robbery highly unlikely though not impossible. Since we do not know the cause of death, it is possible that a robber had some way of killing the men that did not involve injury to their bodies. However, a pathologist did rule out the possibility that the men were injected with something as no injection sites were found on the body (sentence 29).

6. PF; There is enough evidence to make it highly improbable that the two men intentionally killed themselves by ingesting the capsules. Sentence 5 tells us the men were trying to protect themselves from something that they considered dangerous. This indicates a desire to live and not die. Sentence 11 indicates that the men expected to survive taking the capsules since they were supposed to "protect the metals" and "wait for the mask signal" after taking the capsules. Other evidence includes the return ticket for the water bottle that one of the men kept. Why would they

keep a return ticket to return a water bottle if they never intended to return the water bottle? While this in and of itself does not prove that they did not intend to kill themselves, it adds to the weight of the improbable nature of it. In this same vein, we have the fact that the men did buy supplies for their job (sentence 23). Again, why do this if they intend to kill themselves? Then there is the lack of a toxicology report (sentences 27-28). Because of this we have no evidence either way as to whether the cause of death was due to poison, presumably due to the capsules. In fact, we have no evidence that proves that the men took the capsules, though it is likely since they seemed to be following the direction of the note: (1) the time line of the reconstruction of their day indicates they would have arrived at the meeting place around the desired time (and we have one of them anxiously checking his watch at the local bar, which indicates he was anxious about something related to the time), (2) they brought masks, (3) they purchased water in a returnable water bottle—water being desirable for swallowing capsules, and (4) they had the note with them, which seems to indicate they wanted to follow its directions. All of this evidence taken together, makes it probably false that the two men intended to kill themselves when they ingested the capsules.

7. U; While sentence 21 tells us that the location on Vintém Hill where the bodies were found was known for a number of UFO sightings and that a number of locals called the police independently that night to report the same type of UFO, and while Gracinda Barbosa Cortina de Souza and her children claim to have seen a UFO flying over the place where the men died at the time the men were believed to have died (sentence 22), we have no evidence that da Cruz and Viana went to the site to meet aliens. Even if it were true that aliens were in the area, it does not prove that these men expected to meet aliens that night up on that hill.

8. PF; The cause of the men's death is unknown. Sentence 26 tells us that the men died when their hearts stopped (cardiac arrest); however, it is not know why their hearts stopped. Sentences 27-28 tell us that no toxicology report was done and that it was impossible to do later because of the level of decomposition of the organs. This underscores why we cannot know the cause of the men's death, so it is impossible to attribute their death to anyone with certainty, including aliens. There is no evidence that the men went to meet aliens, met aliens, or that aliens were involved in their death. While people in the area reported seeing UFOs, these reports do not prove that the UFOs were caused by aliens or that aliens killed the men. A UFO is simply an unidentified flying object. No one knows what it is, so we cannot make the leap that what people saw that night is proof that aliens exist, that aliens were in the area, or that the men met aliens and were then killed by them. The answer cannot be false because we believe that aliens do not exist. We cannot argue from ignorance; in other words, we cannot conclude that because the existence of aliens hasn't been proved that they then don't exist. There are qualified people on both sides of this issue who claim to have evidence supporting their conclusion. The answer is not unknown because there is a strong likelihood that the men ingested the capsules and that this is what killed them.

B. **Working Hypothesis and Line of Inquiry** (p. 78)

1. **Working hypothesis:** Each detective agency needs a working hypothesis that will guide their investigation. An unknown answer will not work here. A working hypothesis is a proposed explanation that serves as a guide and can change as one investigates and gathers facts. Students must provide their reasoning and state their evidence. The point of this exercise is to have them struggle with the evidence as they use their critical thinking. What is important is not so much

having the "right answer" as it is learning how to evaluate evidence and using reason to construct a working hypothesis.

> **Example of a Working Hypothesis:** The men most likely died accidently from ingesting the capsules.

2. **Reasoning and Evidence:** This is an example of the kind of reasoning and evidence that students need. It goes with the example of a working hypothesis. While there is no evidence that the men actually ingested the capsules since no toxicology report was done, it is highly likely that they did given their behavior in toto: (1) the men were following the directions of the note: they arrived at a predetermined site by the requested time, had masks, and wore them, (2) they were both young men with no evidence at the autopsy of poor health nor any medical reason as to why they both suffered cardiac arrests at about the same time. This leads to the consideration that they had both probably engaged in the same behavior that had the potential to kill them—which was probably ingesting the capsules, (3) their deaths did not occur by violence (sentences 3, 25), and (4) there is no evidence that they intentionally killed themselves; in fact, there is evidence that they intended to survive the evening's activities. So it is a good working hypothesis that they died accidently from ingesting the capsules.

3. **What additional questions would you want answered? Why?** Each agency should have several questions that they would want to pursue in their investigation as well as their reasoning for wanting these questions answered. The purpose of these additional questions is that they help to focus the initial investigation and then move the investigation further along in the same direction or turn it in a new direction depending upon the answers. Of course, new questions would then be generated.

Possible questions: Could someone have given the men the capsules with the intent to murder them? (Reason: to rule murder in or out.) Were the men ignorant of what was in the capsules or the risks associated with the contents of the capsules? (Reason: to prove that their death was accidental and not suicide or murder.) What effect did the men expect would happen when they ingested the capsules? (Reason: to gain a better understanding of what the men were up to, to ascertain if the men were cognizant of what they were doing and the inherent dangers or consequences.) Were the men meeting someone? If so, who? (Reason: to ascertain if there is a witness to what happened or perhaps a person of interest or a possible suspect.) What was supposed to happen after the "mask signal"? Who would give the signal? (Reason: to gain an understanding of what happened up on the hill or what was supposed to happen.) Were the men hoping to buy radioactive material? (Reason: to pursue whether or not the men were involved in an activity that might have led to their death.) If the men did bring a large amount of money with them, then what happened to it? (Reason: to rule robbery in or out with certainty.) Could the men have been killed somewhere else and their bodies dumped at the site on Vintém Hill? (Reason: to determine if where they were found was the original crime scene.)

C. **What Probably Happened to da Cruz and Viana** (p. 79)

The most likely scenario is that the men died accidentally from ingesting whatever was in the capsules. For the evidence, see the *Reasoning and Evidence* answer above. Be open to alternatives if the class can provide sound reasoning and evidence.

Chapter 4
Critical Thinking and Language

4.1   (pages 80-87)

Student Poll (p. 80): Answers will vary. Students need to rate each item in the poll in terms of how the word makes them feel. This poll will be used later in activity #1 of 4.8 Group Activities & Discussion. This activity helps students buy into how language and emotion are related, and in the group activity students will see how language can affect us differently.

Hot, Cold, and Nada Thought Experiment (p. 81): Answers will vary. Students need to complete each of the Hot, Cold, and Nada statements. This activity has students identify why they had a particular emotional reaction, or none at all, to certain words. This activity will also be used in a activity #1 of 4.8 Group Activities & Discussion.

Value Claim Made by Bobby's Dad (p. 82): Bobby is a bad boy.

Student Poll (p. 82): Answers will vary. Students are to rate how easy or hard it is for them to identify the value claim. Then if their rating was any number other than 1 ("Easy"), they are to identify the reason why it was hard for them. Hopefully, they will realize that it is due to the emotionally charged language. This question would be a good way to assess whether the students understand value claims and the power that emotionally charged language can have in terms of obscuring the value claim. As critical thinkers we need to be alert when emotionally charged language is used in an argument since it can obscure the value claim and hook us emotionally so that we overlook whether the arguer provides evidence that supports the conclusion of the argument.

My Prediction (p. 83): Predictions will vary. Students are asked to predict what the caption and image of the turkeys escaping in the shopping cart have to do with critical thinking and the topic of the chapter "Thinking and Language." The connection is to doublespeak, with a nod to gobbledygook.

Emotionally Charged Language Practice I (p. 84): The emotionally charged words are: "filthy," "immoral," and "ruin." If the students identify any other words, then have them make their case for why the words should be considered emotionally charged.

Emotionally Charged Language Practice II (p. 84): Statements #1 and #2 have the students begin to look at the evidence offered in the argument and begin to evaluate it.

1. No, the lyrics of ALL rock music are not "filthy and immoral"; for example, the lyrics of Christian rock music are not "filthy and immoral."

2. No, it is an oversimplification that the lyrics of rock music will by themselves lead to the ruin of society.

3. No, the argument does not provide evidence that actually supports the conclusion that all rock music must be banned. It is false that the lyrics of ALL rock music are "filthy and immoral." An example of why this is false can be found in the lyrics of Christian rock music, which is not "filthy and immoral." Also, the other premise is false; it is an oversimplification that the lyrics of rock music will be the sole cause of the ruin of society.

4. This question asks the student to identify how their emotions were engaged relative to the conclusion, which is due as much to the emotionally charged language as it is to the content of the argument—perhaps even more so.

The cognitive meaning of this argument in neutral language is: The lyrics of rock music have a detrimental (bad) influence on society, so rock music needs to be banned.

The value claim is: Rock music is bad and immoral.

Neutral Words Practice (pp. 85-86): Student answers may vary, but their statements need to capture the meaning in neutral words.   Student answers need to be similar to these:

1. Sam thinks he is very smart (or intelligent).

2. The girl is curious about things that do not concern her.

3. Mr. Jeffers reprimanded me for not doing my homework.

4. My brother is stubborn.

5. The Seattle Mariners are an extremely bad baseball team who make little effort when they play and who, as a result, do not provide a fair value for the hard-earned money spent by fans for their tickets.

Neutral Language & Arguments Practice (p. 86): Student answers may vary, but their arguments need to be in neutral language and reflect the meaning of the word. Student answers need to be similar to these:

1. The lottery should be abolished. The money spent on the lottery is money that is needed to feed children, and it is money needed to pay mortgages and utilities.

2. If you are opposed to cloning organs, then you do not support saving lives. Only someone who does not care about others and lacks compassion would deny people the opportunity to survive. So you need to support research grants for cloning organs.

3. Judy, you need to break up with Charlie. He is not a good boyfriend. He does not care about you, and he has not been faithful. His behavior indicates that he does not love you.

Value Claim Identification Practice (p. 87): The wording may vary in the student answers, but the main idea—and only the main idea—of the value claim needs to be evident. If student answers have more content than the value claim, then it means that the students were not able to focus in on the value claim and identify it.

1. The lottery is bad and hurts people.

2. Opposing cloning is immoral.

3. Charlie is a bad person.

Check-in (p. 87): These self-assessments are important for the students. If any of them have selected the little dog in the Superman costume, then encourage them to seek coaching on how to identify value claims in arguments.

4.2   (pages 88-93)

The "Why" of Understanding Language Practice (p. 88): Understanding language is important for us as critical thinkers. Here's an example of the "Why" as it might appear on the placard:

Understanding language is important for:

- Communicating effectively.
- Understanding how words hook us emotionally & disengage our reason.
- Creating & evaluating arguments.
- Preventing being tricked or misled.

The "Say What?" Thought Experiment (p. 89): The student answers will vary, but here are some possible responses.

1. pen: noun – an enclosure; a writing implement; a female swan; a protected dock for a submarine; penitentiary; verb – to shut in; to write

2. bank: noun – mound or ridge above the surrounding level; piled-up mass of clouds or fog; steep slope; a supply of something in reserve; an establishment for the custody, loan, or issue of money or credit; depot for the collection or storage of human biological product (e.g., blood bank); verb – to raise a bank about, to cover (a fire) with fresh fuel and adjust the draft of air, drive (a ball in billiards) into a cushion, to incline laterally

3. suit: noun – an action or process in court for the recovery of a right or claim; an appeal in a courtship; set of garments that is made of the same material and consists of a skirt or pair of pants and a jacket; all the playing cards in a pack bearing the same symbols; slang for a business executive; verb – to dress; to please; to be becoming (e.g., the dress suits you); to be appropriate

4. hard: noun – not easily penetrated; firm; factual; searching (e.g, gave a hard look); lacking compassion or gentleness; difficult to endure; unrelenting; difficulty doing something (e.g., hard of hearing); difficult to accomplish

5. critical: noun – crucial or decisive; inclined to criticize; sufficient size to sustain a critical reaction

6. race: noun – act of running; strong or rapid current of water flowing through a narrow channel; a set course or duration of time; breed; contest of speed; family tribe of people or nation united by shared interest, habits, or characteristics; category of humankind that share certain distinctive physical traits; verb – to compete in a race; to enter into a race; to move or function at top speed or out of control

Two Different Meanings of "Visiting relatives can be boring." (p. 90)

1. Relatives who visit can be boring.

2. Going to visit relatives can be boring.

Prediction Revision (p. 90): Now that students have had the experience with predictions in chapter 1 and 3, they know what to expect. It might be fun to add some incentive to this activity once in a while, such as having them list their predictions on a chart and see how accurate they are in relation to one another. The opportunity for revision will encourage them to reflect on what they have already learned and do some creative thinking and creative problem solving—which is what the picture will introduce.

Ambiguity in Statements (p. 91): For each example, students need to bracket the two meanings of the statement and then provide the meaning of each statement. Students may do these in any order, though they must have these answers.

Example 2:

    a. Milk drinkers are turning [to powder.]
       Meaning: They are drinking powdered milk.

    b. Milk drinkers [are turning to powder.]
       Meaning: They are turning into powder.

Example 3:

    a. Enraged cow injures [farmer with ax.]
       Meaning: The cow hurt the farmer who had the ax.

    b. [Enraged cow injures] farmer [with ax.]
       Meaning: The cow used the ax to hurt the farmer.

Ambiguity and Real-life Headlines Practice (p. 93): The students need to provide two alternate meanings of the headlines and then make a choice as to which meaning is the most likely and explain why. Student answers will not necessary match what we have here for an "a" answer or "b" answer etc. The use of "a" etc. is for a way to discuss the possible meanings and the one that is the most likely. In some cases, there are more than two possible meanings. Students only need to provide two, but they need to make every effort to provide the one that is actually the most likely.

1. The possible meanings are: a. The bill would allow putting ads onto eyeglasses. b. The bill would allow advertising of eyeglasses. c. Some guy named Bill would allow putting ads on eyeglasses. d. Some guy named Bill would allow advertising of eyeglasses.
    Most likely meaning: b. The bill would allow advertising of eyeglasses.
    The Why: Meaning "a" is not likely since no permission would be needed to place advertising on any portion of the glasses, such as the ear pieces, though it is highly unlikely that ads would be placed on the lens since that would affect vision. Meanings "c" and "d" are unlikely because why is permission needed from some unknown individual named "Bill"—unknown since his last name is not stated—to put ads on eyeglasses or to advertise selling glasses. If someone famous, who had a line of glasses, was going to allow advertising on their glasses, then the headline would surely state the person's full name. The most likely choice is "b," Opticians will be permitted to advertise.

2. The possible meanings are: a. The chef physically throws his actual heart into the food that he feeds the needy people. b. The chef is passionate about helping feed needy people.
    Most likely meaning: b. The chef is passionate about helping feed needy people.
    The Why: Meaning "a" is impossible: how can the chef, who is alive, literally take out his heart and put it into the food that will feed the needy people (and really, would they want to eat a human

heart?). So the most like choice is "b"—that he really cares about feeding people who are economically disadvantaged—hungry people who struggle to make ends meet—and he takes action to do that.

3. The possible meanings are: a. The tree found the stolen painting. b. The painting was found next to the tree. Most likely meaning: b. The painting was found next to the tree.
   The Why: Meaning "a" is impossible given our reality on Earth—trees, while alive—do not walk around finding things. So "b" is the most likely meaning.

4. Possible meanings: a. A man who was eating a piranha was mistakenly sold as a pet fish. b. A man-eating piranha was mistakenly sold as a pet fish. c. A man was eating a piranha that was mistakenly sold as a pet fish.
   Most likely meaning: b. A man-eating piranha was mistakenly sold as a pet fish.
   The Why: Despite the possibility that a man might eat a piranha, human beings are not mistaken for a fish, so meaning "a" doesn't make sense. While it is possible that a man was eating a piranha that was mistakenly sold as a pet fish (meaning c), it is not as likely as meaning b. The ambiguity could have been avoided if the compound adjective describing the piranha had been spelled correctly: "Man-eating."

4.3   (pages 94-98)

The Broccoli Thought Experiment (p. 94): It isn't clear from the statement how much broccoli the child would actually have to eat in order to get dessert. The phrase "a little more" is vague, and what the child, especially one who doesn't like broccoli, thinks is "a little more" and what the mother thinks is "a little more" will probably be different. The child will want to eat as little of the broccoli as possible while the mother will want the child to eat as much as she can get the child to eat. It is highly unlikely that they are thinking of the same amount.

Student Poll (p. 95): Answers will vary. What the poll is intended to show is that there are borderline cases where we aren't sure if the word applies or not due to the vagueness of the word. It should be easy to pick those who are obviously rich and those who are not, but it is much harder to identify those cases that are "iffy."

Reason for Different Answers (p. 95): The variety of answers that the students may see in their poll will be due to people's own life experiences around the word "rich." The answers would more than likely be much different if people from different socioeconomic strata were polled.

Writing a Law (p. 95): If we were writing a law that would apply specifically to people who were rich, then we would need to be very precise about what "rich" means, so we would need a "precising definition." Precising definitions are used to make words very clear by making the definition as precise as possible, and they are important for resolving disputes over the meaning of words. In our example of who is rich, a precising definition might define someone as rich if the person earns over $400,000 a year before taxes and has a net worth of one million dollars or more. This would make it clear who is rich or not.

Vagueness Practice (p. 97)

1. Vague; vague term: "loads"; We would need to know how many people were actually at the game, or if this is in a causal conversation, at least be less vague, such as saying there were "about 350 people."

2. Not vague.

3. Vague; Vague phrase: "more or less done"; We would need to know what work still needs to be done to complete the homework.

4. Vague; Vague term: "excessive"; We would need a precise definition of "excessive" so that we could evaluate whether or not paying $100 is excessive. There may be disagreement over the definition of "excessive."

5. Vague; Vague phrase: "skin like peaches and cream"; We need to know what this phrase means and how using the product makes our skin "like peaches and cream." As discerning consumers, we need to evaluate this claim for its veracity.

6. Not vague (the facts listed in the statement are true).

4.4   (pages 99-105)

Doublespeak Thought Experiment   (p. 99)

1. e; 2. d; 3. h; 4. i; 5. j; 6. a; 7. f; 8. g; 9. b; 10. c.

Class discussion of the doublespeak found in this Thought Experiment will open the door for students sharing other doublespeak they have encountered and will encourage buy-in.

Food Insecurity Questions (p. 101): Answers will vary. These questions have students look closely at the use of doublespeak and how it affects and shapes reality. Students will have the opportunity to share their answers in activity #4 in 4.8 Group Activities & Discussion. If students have not completed these questions, then give the class time to review their answers or complete them so that they can participate in the discussion.

Student Poll (p. 102): Answers will vary. Death as a topic was selected because of the sheer volume of euphemisms that surround it. In the American culture, direct talk about death is basically taboo; hence the euphemisms. This poll will be the basis of activity #5 in 4.8 Group Activities & Discussion. It also provides an excellent place to make sure that students understand what doubletalk is and how and why it operates in our culture.

Doublespeak Practice (p. 104): Besides identifying the euphemism, students are to explain whether or not the pair of statements has the same emotional impact on them and why. This practice will be the basis of activity #6 in 4.8 Group Activities & Discussion about the impact of doublespeak on individuals and "the why" of it.

1. a. uninstalled; 2. a. decommissioned aggressor quantum; 3. b. revenue enhancement;
4. b. previously distinguished; 5. a. terminal living; 6. b. encore telecasts

Notice that in each case the use of doublespeak is used to misdirect and even manipulate feelings: "uninstalled" depersonalizes what occurs and attempts to gut the emotional impact, and even our comprehension of the consequences, of the act; "decommissioned aggressor quantum" dehumanizes who is killed—what is a "quantum"?—whereas we do know that soldiers are human beings like us; "revenue enhancement" doesn't sound bad; in fact, the use of the word "enhancement" is a positive word and is used to mislead people that what is occurring is really an increase in taxes; "previously distinguished" also misleads people and attempts to bypass any negative feelings or concerns we have associated with used cars.

4.5   (pages 106-110)

Gobbledygook Thought Experiment (p. 106): Answers will vary. The students are to attempt to translate this quote by Alan Greenspan into neutral language. They should not feel bad if they can't because no one else has been able to either! The point of this activity is to struggle with real-life gobbledygook and experience first-hand the problem of assigning meaning, if there is any, to it.

Your Turn Thought Experiment (p. 108): Answers will vary. Students get to create their own gobbledygook based on the statement "Students are not allowed to have hot drinks in the classroom." Every student is expected to come up with an answer, though some will be much more imaginative than others. One possible answer is "Individuals who are involved in educational activities within a space dedicated to the interaction between a person hired to impart knowledge and said individuals are enjoined against holding, using, imbibing, or having contact with liquids that are capable of giving a sensation of heat in the aforementioned space at any time." If students ask how to write gobbledygook, suggest that they look up words in a dictionary, a learner's dictionary, or a thesaurus.

Student Poll   (p. 108)
1. desks
2. grocery store checkout clerks
3. junkyard
4. elevator operators

The "I Spy" Thought Experiment (p. 110): Answers will vary. Students need to identify ways to recognize doublespeak and what is actually being said as well as how not to be fooled by it. Then they are to create a PSA, or public service announcement, to help people their own age understand what doublespeak is and how not to be fooled by it. This activity has students use all of the cognitive skills we looked at in section 1.1: comprehension, analysis, evaluation, construction, creativity, and communication. This activity will be the foundation of activity #8 in 4.8 Group Activities & Discussion.

Student Poll (p. 110): Answers will vary Students are to read the story and rate the level of critical thinking going on in the story. This enables them to use several critical thinking skills, such as comprehension and evaluation.

4.6   (pages 111-113)

Important Takeaways (p. 113): The students need to think about what they learned in this chapter and identify three takeaways that are important to them for their life. This activity makes the content of the chapter personally relevant to them. Small group or large group discussion about their takeaways would demonstrate to the students the various ways that the content of the chapter was relevant to people in the class.

4.7   (pages 114-117)

1. **Using Neutral Language** (p. 114): Answers will vary in terms of how the arguments are rewritten in neutral language, but they must convey the cognitive meaning of the argument and the value claim. These are two examples of how the arguments could be restated in neutral language.

   a. Video games cause an increase in the violent behavior of young people. This violent behavior leads to murder and other criminal activities. Therefore, it should be illegal for children under the age of eighteen to be able to buy or watch video games.

      Value claim: Video games are bad.

   b. It should be legal to reproduce and share unauthorized copies of music CDs because the artists are multimillionaires who overcharge adults and children who do not have an excess of money to spend. Moreover, it reduces pollution because fewer CDs will end up in landfills.

      Value claims: It is not immoral to reproduce and share unauthorized copies of music CDs. The artists, who are very wealthy, are immoral for overcharging for their music.

2. **Testing for Ambiguity and Vagueness** (p. 115)
   a. No problem
   b. Problem, vague; "rich"
   c. No problem
   d. Problem; ambiguity; "lack of brains"
   e. Problem; ambiguity; "Eats anything and is especially fond of children." (The ambiguity is due to the entire phrase.)
   f. Problem; vague; "excessive."

3. **Headlines** (p. 116): The students need to provide two alternate meanings of the headlines and then make a choice as to which meaning is more likely, explaining why.

   a. The lawyers have returned despite the use of bug spray to prevent them from returning.   OR Despite the use of bug spray in the area of their building, the lawyers have returned. The likely meaning is that despite the use of bug spray in the area of their building (in this case bug spray sprayed in the Prosecutor's Office), the lawyers have returned.

   b. Police took possession of 14 elephants who had fake IDs. OR The police used fake IDs to take possession of 14 elephants. The likely meaning is that the police used fake IDs to take possession of 14 elephants. (It may even be likely that the real meaning is that the police seized the elephants along with some fake IDs in their raid. The meaning would only become clear after reading the story.)

4. **Name the Doublespeak** (p. 117)
   a. inflated language
   b. euphemism
   c. inflated language
   d. jargon
   e. jargon
   f. inflated language

4.8   (pages 118-119)

1. **Hot, Cold, and Nada** (p. 118): Answers will vary. Students will see that not everyone has the same emotional response to the words as they do, which is due to the personal experiences they've had that have been associated with some of these words. They will also begin to identify how emotionally charged language is used in their culture, such as to persuade them to do something or to elect someone or to sell them products.

2. **Neutral Language and Value Claims** (p. 118): See answers to activity #1 in 4.7. Identifying the value claims may be the most difficult part of this activity, especially since there are two value claims being made in b. It is important that students see how value claims can be obscured by emotionally charged language.

3. **Doublespeak Thought Experiment** (p. 118): Answers will vary. Students need to understand the intent behind doublespeak. It is used to mislead people and to distort reality. William Lutz, an authority on doublespeak, explains that people who use doublespeak are trying to shift responsibility and "make the bad seem good, the negative appear positive, something unpleasant appear attractive … It is language designed to alter our perception of reality and corrupt our thinking. Such language does not provide us with the tools we need to develop, advance, and preserve our culture and our civilization. Such language breeds suspicion, cynicism, distrust, and, ultimately, hostility."[1] He notes that when language is corrupted, it damages communication, affects people's thinking, and reshapes reality. He also points out how it can impact the thinking and the choices of an electorate that is misinformed due to doublespeak. It is important that critical thinkers are able to identify doublespeak when they run into it and figure out what is actually being said. Failing to identify doublespeak is one sign of how pervasive it is and how reality is already being shaped.

4. **MSNBC Hunger Crisis** (p. 118): This example of the use of "food insecurity" demonstrates to the students how doublespeak can shape reality and how pervasive it can be in our culture. For MSNBC to use it in the way that they did assumes that it is a term that is commonly accepted and used and not merely jargon. This term reshapes people's view of the reality of the problem of hunger in the United States as well as impacting the emotional response people have to the situation facing millions of Americans. In effect, it abstracts the problem, whereas the word "hunger" concretizes the problem since all of us have had some experience with how it feels to be hungry. The phase "fell victim" does pull the reader back in emotionally and facilitates empathy for those who face hunger on a daily basis. However, the impact of this phrase is undercut by the euphemism "food insecurity."

5. **Student Poll on Death** (p. 118): Other euphemisms for death from a medical context include "substantive negative outcome," "negative patient-care outcome," "therapeutic misadventure," and "failed to fulfill his wellness potential." These are good examples of how doublespeak abstracts something concrete and attempts to gut the negative impact of death. The term "therapeutic misadventure" was used by a hospital when an anesthesiologist made a mistake that killed a patient. Notice how it minimizes the mistake. The patient's family probably did not experience her "therapeutic misadventure" in quite the same way. The last example, "failed to fulfill his wellness potential," was written on a patient's chart by the doctor after he died. This would be a great example to share with students, asking them what kind of emotional response it elicits versus saying the patient died. Ask

---

1. William Lutz, "The World of Doublespeak," *The Brief Bedford Reader*, 9th ed., eds. X. J. Kennedy, Dorothy M. Kennedy, and Jane E. Aaron (Boston: Bedford/St. Martin's, 2006), 353.

them too if it blames the man for his own death, and how it might make them view death. Doublespeak like this is intentional and should lead us to ask why it is being used. The other examples in this activity will help facilitate an interesting and lively discussion.

6. **Doublespeak Practice** (p. 119): See the answers for section 4.4. This activity could be combined with activity #4.

7. **Gobbledygook** (p. 119): This activity is a fun way to emphasize the problem of gobbledygook and to help students identify it when they see it. Follow up with a discussion about why someone might want to use gobbledygook. Reasons for its use include (1) wanting to mislead or misdirect, (2) wanting to appear important or an expert, (3) failing to understand the subject matter and consequently saying nothing, and (4) being a poor communicator. Encourage the small groups to make use of a dictionary or thesaurus if they need help writing their gobbledygook.

8. **Public Service Announcement (PSA)** (p. 119): The Public Service Announcement (PSA) makes use of all of the cognitive skills discussed in chapter one. This can be a project for the class that can be shared with their school. This allows them to apply what they are learning and reinforces the learning as they teach others.

Chapter 5
Analyzing Arguments

5.1   (pages 120-121)

Student Poll (p. 120): Answers will vary. This poll shows students that they run into arguments everywhere and from people all around them, including making arguments themselves. The score that students apply to how often they make an argument will reveal how conscious they are of trying to persuade others through arguments. This could serve as a good discussion starter about their use of arguments and, in the process, foster buy-in to the study of arguments.

Of Monsters and Men Practice   (p. 121)

The conclusion of the argument (and what Scott is trying to persuade his parents to allow him to do):   I should be allowed to go with my friends Kevin and Greg to see Of Monsters and Men.

The three premises of the argument are:

1. I'm 17 years old and very responsible.

2. I've never missed my curfew or gotten into trouble and neither has Kevin or Greg.

3. I've kept up my grades all semester.

5.2   (pages 122-128)

The Two Kinds of Statements That Make Up an Argument (p. 122): conclusion; premises.

Operator and Assertion Practice   (p. 124)

1. The two operators are "or" and "and."

2. There are three assertions in the second premise.

3. The three assertions are: (1) "I've never missed my curfew," (2) "I've never gotten into trouble," and (3) "Kevin and Greg have never missed their curfew or gotten into trouble."

More Argument Practice   (p. 124)

Conclusion: Indie folk music is the best.

Premise 1: The artists don't sell out—they're an independent rock community.

Premise 2: They also combine folk music and classic country music with indie rock to create a unique sound.

My Prediction (p. 125): Predictions will vary. In this prediction students must predict what a fortune teller making a prediction has to do with learning about arguments. The tie-in is to inductive arguments because the fortune teller actually makes a predictive argument, which is a type of inductive argument.

Your Argument Thought Experiment (p. 126): Answers will vary. Students are connecting their real-life experience making arguments with their study of arguments in this chapter and with critical thinking in general. They will learn to identify the conclusion of their argument as well as the premises. Later they and the other students will evaluate their arguments as a part of activity #2 in 5.10 Group Activities & Discussion. It may be necessary to select one or two of the students' arguments to use as an example to work with if some students are having difficulty identifying the premises.

Statement Practice (p. 127)

The statements are 1, 2, 5, 6 8, 10, 11. Additional information about the truth value of each statement is provided as well as identification of the type of sentences that occur in this activity which are not statements.

1. Statement; The truth of this statement can be determined by checking whether or not it is raining outside.

2. Statement; This statement is true.

3. Not a statement; It is a command.

4. Not a statement; It is an exclamation.

5. Statement; This statement is true.

6. Statement; This statement is false. Sally Ride was the first U.S. woman in space.

7. Not a statement; It is a suggestion.

8. Statement; It is true.

9. Not a statement; It is a suggestion.

10. Statement; It is true.

11. Statement. It is true. While Mr. Spock is not a real person, he is a character whose background and lineage has been developed and can be checked from information about Star Trek.

Conclusion Practice (pp. 127-128)

1. A rose must be pretty. Conclusion indicator word: "so."

2. A rhinoceros is not a vegetable. Premise indicator word: "because."

3. All birds must be black. Conclusion indicator word: "therefore."

4. You cannot step twice in the same river. Premise indicator word: "for."

5. Mr. Ed is a mammal. Conclusion indicator word: "hence."

6. Beyoncé is probably a millionaire. Premise indicator: "since."

7. Some girls play sports. Conclusion indicator: "therefore."

8. Dogs aren't as smart as cats. There are no indicator words.

9. We should quit publishing books. Conclusion indicator word: "consequently."

10. Everyone should be encouraged to eat ice cream. Conclusion indicator word: "it follows that."

5.3 (pages 129-133)

The Dog in the Rubble Thought Experiment (p. 129): Answers will vary.

My Argument: Students are to read the story and then create an argument based in some way on the story; for example, they might argue that it is important to look for a lost pet after a natural disaster for more than a week since it is possible for them to survive for longer than expected, or that animal rescue organizations do important work, or that hot dogs are a great food since they can serve many useful purposes, or that when dogs wag their tails they are happy, or that it is important to have a pet evacuation plan when facing natural disasters like tornados. The students will have an opportunity to work with each other's argument in activity #3 of 5.10 Group Activities & Discussion. If students have difficulty developing an argument, then provide them with a few suggestions.

Conclusion and Premise(s): Once students write their arguments, then they are to identify the conclusion and each of their premises.

Was It Obvious: Students are to reflect on whether or not they could tell if the passage was an argument and their reason why. This will lay the groundwork and facilitate buy-in to the discussion around what an argument is and what are the types of nonarguments that they are already familiar with.

An Argument is Made Up of This (p. 130): 2; conclusion, premise(s).

An Inferential Relationship Means (p. 130): That at least one statement (the premise[s]) must claim to provide evidence or reasons for another statement (conclusion).

"To Be Or Not To Be" Practice (p. 132)

1. Not an argument; A single conditional statement is never an argument.

2. Not an argument; Neither an opinion nor a statement of belief is an argument.

3. Argument; This is an argument from example and not an illustration. The conclusion is: Cats run faster than dogs.

4. Not an argument; This is a news report.

5. Argument; The conclusion is: Sally Ride deserves to receive a national tribute. The other statements are premises.

6. This is not an argument; This is an explanation. The passage is explaining why Eva Hesse is considered one of the most innovative artists of the postwar period.

7. Argument; The conclusion is: A state of emergency needs to be declared because of the massive amount of sea lion pups that are starving. The other two statements are premises.

8. Argument. This argument makes use of conditional statements. The conclusion is: If Harry doesn't win the next 800m run, he will lose his scholarship.

5.4   (pages 134-139)

The Beatles Thought Experiment (p. 134): Answers will vary. This activity has the students look closely at the two different types of arguments (deductive and inductive arguments) and evaluate them in terms of their differences. The goal is to get them to notice the difference between the inferential relationships in the two arguments. They also are asked to decide which one is more convincing to them and why. This is another way of getting at the difference in the inferential relationships in the two arguments.

An Inferential Relationship Is (p. 134): a special relationship in which at least one statement (the premise[s]) must claim to provide evidence or reasons for another statement (the conclusion).

Student Poll (p. 135): Argument 1 has the strongest inferential relationship between the conclusion and the premises.

Prediction Revision (p. 135): Students have an opportunity to think about how the prediction might relate to arguments. They have now studied arguments and their form, and they should be able to identify that what the fortune teller says is actually an argument—a predictive argument. They are also able to evaluate this argument and see that it is not a deductive argument since there is no guarantee of the truth of the conclusion. So, what we have is an inductive argument—one that makes a prediction—which provides only the probability of the truth of the conclusion.

The Clues Quiz (p. 138): Students should have checked: form of the argument; words like certainty or definitely (which are deductive indicator words); actual strength of the relationship between the premises and the conclusion.

Deductive Argument Form Practice   (pp. 138-139)

1. Disjunctive syllogism; Conclusion: Harold will get his driver's license by April 15th.

2. Argument from definition; Conclusion: There is a special closeness between them.

3. Hypothetical syllogism; Conclusion: The University of Oregon did not beat Oregon State University.

4. Categorical Syllogism; Conclusion: All protons have mass.

5. Hypothetical syllogism; Conclusion: If a dangerous weather system brings white-out conditions and below zero temperature, I will be so bummed out.

5.5   (pages 140-149)

Student Poll (p. 141): The inferential claim is stronger in the deductive argument than in the inductive argument. In a deductive argument the conclusion follows with strict necessity from the premises, but in an inductive argument the conclusion follows only with probability.   So on the left side: inductive argument; on the right side: deductive argument.

The Apples Argument   (pp. 141-142):

Conclusion (p. 141): The other six apples in the basket will probably be delicious too.

Premise (p.141): The eight apples I took from the basket my aunt gave me were delicious.

Indicator word (p. 141): since – Students needed to circle "since" in the argument.

Strength of the inferential relationship (p. 142): No. There is no guarantee that the other six apples in the basket will be delicious. There is only the probability that they will be delicious because eight others were delicious. The probability increases that the other apples will be delicious as the number of delicious apples eaten increases. However, the probability decreases if I have eaten fewer apples than eight. This means that my argument will get weaker. In fact, with each fewer apple eaten, the argument weakens more. Think of it as a kind of sliding scale.

Argument From Authority Thought Experiment   (p. 144)

The first argument: The authority is Mr. O'Toole. He is an authority because he is an eyewitness to the murder. We do not have a guarantee of the truth of the conclusion because it is possible for an eyewitness to make a mistake. Evidence of this is seen in the release of individuals convicted of murder based on eyewitness testimony that proves later to be incorrect. The Innocence Project indicates eyewitness misidentification as the number one cause of wrongful convictions in the United States. In fact, eyewitness misidentification has played a role in 75% of the convictions overturned through DNA testing. Because of this we only have probability regarding the truth that Thomas committed the murder.

The second argument: The authority is Dr. Hart. He is an authority because he is a doctor, specifically a cardiologist dealing with a heart problem. There is no guarantee of the truth of the conclusion that the speaker needs a pacemaker because it is possible that Dr. Hart made a mistake. Doctors are not infallible, even the outstanding ones, and do make mistakes.

Deductive vs. Inductive Practice   (p. 147)

	Deductive or Inductive	Form of Argument	Deductive/Inductive Indicator Words
1.	inductive	predictive argument	probably
2.	inductive	causal argument	reasonable to conclude
3.	deductive	hypothetical syllogism	necessarily follows
4.	inductive	argument from analogy	none

"The Why" Argument Practice (p. 148)

	Deductive or Inductive	Deductive/Inductive Indicator Words	Inferential Relationship	Form of Argument
1.	deductive	none	strict necessity	argument from definition
2.	inductive	probably	probability	inductive generalization
3.	deductive	none	strict necessity	categorical syllogism
4.	deductive	none	strict necessity	hypothetical syllogism
5.	deductive	none	strict necessity	disjunctive syllogism
6.	inductive	none	probability	causal argument

5.6   (pages 150-151)

The "Dogs Really Do Surf!" Thought Experiment (pp. 150-151): Answers will vary. This exercise is to prime students for the discussion on evaluating arguments that will come. Students need to identify who they believe has the most convincing argument and why. Then they identify who doesn't have the most convincing argument and why. They also need to explain their criteria for evaluating the argument. Students will take a second look at these arguments in small groups in activity #4 in 5.10 Group Activities & Discussion and then as a larger group.

Testing for a Valid Argument Practice   (p. 153)

Example 1: Yes, valid
Example 2: Yes, valid
Example 3: No, not valid (so invalid)
Example 4: Yes, valid.

Testing for a Valid Argument Example 1 Using Diagram (p. 154): Yes, Cranberry Sweets belongs to the circle of companies that manufacture candy. Yes, the circle of companies who manufactures candy belongs to the circle of all companies that manufacture food. Because we have the two "Yes" answers, then Cranberry Sweets is a company that manufactures food. So we have a valid argument.

Testing for a Valid Argument Example 3 Using Diagram (p. 155): The red circle (apples) is in the yellow circle (fruit) and not in the green circle (vegetables), so there is no way for apples to be vegetables. This means it is possible that we can have true premises and a false conclusion, so the argument is invalid.

Testing for a Sound Argument Examples 1 and 2   (p. 156)

	Valid argument?	Sound argument?
Example 1	yes	yes
Example 2	yes	no

Testing for Soundness Practice I   (p. 157)

	Valid argument?	All premises true?	Sound argument?	Reason?
Example 3	no	Invalid argument—no need to evaluate premises.	no	invalid argument
Example 4	yes	No. Both premises not true. Once identify one false premise, no need to check the other one.	no	at least one premise is not true

Check-in (p. 158): Students need to continue to do these self-assessments. Continue to encourage them to get coaching if they need it from a teacher or another student. Tie this to critical thinking: critical thinkers know when to seek help so that they can become proficient with the material they are studying. Poor critical thinking results in denial and avoidance of the problem.

Testing for Soundness Practice II (p. 160):

	Valid argument?	All true premises?	Sound argument?	Explanation
1.	yes	no	no	*Harry Potter and the Sorcerer's Stone* was written by J.K. Rowling and not Shakespeare. Once we have one premise with a false truth value, then we do not need to check any other premise.
2.	yes	yes	yes	
3.	no	yes	no	This case is the one exception when content comes into play when evaluating an argument for validity—in actuality we have true premises with a false conclusion. This makes it invalid immediately due to the definition of an invalid argument.
4.	yes	yes	yes	
5.	yes	no	no	The second premise is false. Lee Harvey Oswald shot President Kennedy, not President Lincoln. John Wilkes Booth shot President Lincoln.
6.	yes	yes	yes	
7.	no	n/a	no	Since the argument is invalid, there is no reason to evaluate the premises.
8.	yes	no	no	*Saturday Night Live* is a comedy; it is not a drama.

5.7   (pages 162-174)

The Surfing Goats Thought Experiment (pp. 162-163): Answers will vary. Students need to identify who they believe has the most convincing argument and why. Then they identify who doesn't have the most convincing argument and why. They also need to explain their criteria for evaluating the argument. Students will take a second look at the three friends' arguments in activity #5 in 5.10 Group Activities & Discussion, which involves small group discussion and large group discussion.

The Claims Quiz (p. 164)

Factual claim: a
Inferential claim: b
Test first: Inferential claim
Test second: Factual claim

Test the Inferential Claim First (p. 164): Always test the inferential claim first because if the premises do not support the conclusion, then the argument is defective in reasoning and has no value.

Stage 1: When We Have a Weak Argument (p. 165): If we have a weak argument, then we do not need to continue evaluating the argument because there is no way for it to be cogent. One of the requirements for having a cogent argument is to have a strong argument. Another way to explain this is that with a weak argument the premises do not provide the necessary support for the conclusion, and what we want and need is for the premises to provide that support, even though in an inductive argument the premises provide only the probability of the truth of the conclusion.

Testing For A Strong Argument Practice (p. 167)

Example 1: strong
Example 2: strong
Example 3: weak
Example 4: strong

Harder or Easier? (p. 167): Answers will vary. Students need to decide if it was harder or easier to test the inductive arguments for whether they were strong or weak in comparison to testing deductive arguments for validity. This question is getting them to compare the inferential claim for inductive and deductive arguments. Is it harder or easier to check the inferential claim when looking at an inductive argument versus a deductive argument? Some students will say it is neither harder nor easier. Have them explain why. This choice was not given in order to force students to look closely at what they are doing. For some people it is easier to check for necessity over probability while for others it makes no difference because the process is basically the same, though it can be difficult for some students to learn.

Example 2 – Type of Inductive Argument (p. 167): Argument from Analogy

Example 3 – Type of Inductive Argument (p. 168): Argument from Authority

Check-in (p. 170): There is a second check-in due to the difficulty of the chapter. We don't want students to fall behind in terms of understanding the material. If this happens, then they may feel very overwhelmed. Consider offering some portion of a class period as a coaching session. Put students in small groups and have them review the material together as you circulate to offer additional help. Or consider setting aside a portion of a class period to let students work on homework for this class while you open a "coaching center" manned by a few selected students who can answer questions as you circulate the room to help those who might be embarrassed to come and ask for help at a "coaching center." It cannot be overemphasized that as critical thinkers we need to know when we need help and ask for it. There is no shame in that; in fact, it is a sign of great critical thinking.

Testing for a Cogent Argument Practice I (p. 171)

	Strong argument?	All true premises?	Key evidence ignored that requires a different conclusion?	Cogent argument?	Explanation
Example 2	yes	yes	no	yes	
Example 3	no	n/a	n/a	no	Weak argument; no need to evaluate further.
Example 4	yes	no	n/a	no	Premise 2 is not true: Justin Bieber is not a senator. No need to evaluate further.

Checking for a Cogent Argument Practice II (p. 173)

	Strong argument?	All true premises?	Key evidence ignored that requires a different conclusion?	Cogent argument?	Explanation
1.	no	n/a	n/a	no	Weak argument; no need for further evaluation. This is an argument from analogy. While there are some similarities, the disanalogy between the universe and a pocket watch is too great. Nature is not like a machine, and quantum mechanics (a theory in physics that explains the behavior of atoms and other minute systems) has unpredictability built into it. This is not the orderly, predictable world of machines. String theory[2] suggests an even greater degree of unpredictability. This is a much more dynamic and complex view of reality than a predictable, mechanistic one suggested by the analogy likening the universe to a pocket watch.

2. String theory, which was first introduced in 1970, proposes a new way to view the composition of reality that includes vibrating string and membranes (branes) of energy, extra dimensions, and multiple universes. These other dimensions, which are crumpled up so small in size that they are hard to detect, affect the physical features of each universe, so every universe is different. These universes exist on branes that are strings that are stretched out and parallel to one another.

	Strong argument?	All true premises?	Key evidence ignored that requires a different conclusion?	Cogent argument?	Explanation
2.	no	n/a	n/a	no	This is a weak argument from analogy, so there is no need for further evaluation. The disanalogy between human models and mannequins is too great to make this a strong argument.
3.	yes	yes	no	yes	
4.	yes	no	n/a	no	The weather year round in Honolulu, Hawaii, is not always cold with the majority of days snowing. It is common knowledge that Hawaii is a tropical, warm state. Even during the cold season at the location of the Bowl Game there is an average high of 81 degrees and a low of 66 degrees, and it is exceptionally unlikely for snow to occur. There is no need for further evaluation.
5.	yes	yes	no	yes	The picture, caption, and fact information contain all the information necessary to evaluate the truth of the premises.

5.8   (pages 175-178)

Important Takeaways (p. 178): The students need to focus on what three takeaways from this chapter on arguments are relevant to their lives. A large group discussion will help facilitate everyone's buy-in to struggling with the concepts in the chapter. Consider framing the conversation in terms of the importance of the chapter's content to critical thinking.

5.9   (pages 179-181)

Officer on Duty

1. Inductive; strong; no; Not cogent due to a false premise.

2. Deductive argument; valid; yes; sound.

3. Deductive argument; invalid; No need to check the premises because the argument is invalid, but in actuality it has a true premise and a false conclusion which also makes the argument invalid; not sound.

4. Deductive argument; valid; yes; sound.

5. Deductive argument; invalid; No need to check the premises because the argument is invalid, but in actuality it has a true premise and a false conclusion which also makes the argument invalid; not sound.

6. Deductive argument; valid; yes; sound.

7. Inductive argument; strong; yes; cogent.

8. Inductive argument; strong; yes; cogent.

5.10   (pages 182-185)

1. **Should Scott Go?** (p. 182): Deductive argument; valid; no; not sound due to a false premise: "I've never missed my curfew or gotten into trouble and neither has Kevin or Greg." It is not true that Greg has never gotten into trouble. He got into trouble last year tagging a building, though he hasn't gotten into trouble since then. Scott could have made a sound argument by changing this premise and adding an additional one: "I've never missed my curfew or gotten into trouble and neither has Kevin. Greg has turned things around and hasn't gotten into trouble at all this year." As a class discuss whether or not Scott had a convincing argument. Should he be allowed to go? Why or why not?

2. **Our Evaluation** (pp. 182-183): These answers will vary. The teacher needs to circulate to review the evaluations, making sure the students understand and can apply what they have learned about evaluating arguments. As a large group work through the sampling of the arguments (this sampling comes from the arguments that have been self-identified by the small groups). Important to this discussion is how to make the arguments that are not sound or cogent into sound or cogent arguments.

3. **Dog in the Rubble** (p. 184): This follows the same process as in problem #2, except that the small groups will have the opportunity to consider what to do to make any arguments that are not sound or cogent into sound or cogent arguments. If they have difficulties doing this, then encourage them to select the argument to use in the large group discussion.

4. **Surfing Dogs** (p. 184): Students may have some difficulty identifying the main premises since there are subarguments and counterarguments. Because this is a basic introduction to arguments, there is not a discussion about subarguments or counterarguments. We have tried to simplify the topic and have the students identify the main conclusion being made by the arguers and the premises that support this. An example of a subargument: "It isn't safe for dogs to surf because they could drown." Rick's comment that "they could drown" is a premise (reason) as to why it isn't safe for dogs to surf. Another example of a subargument occurs when Stacy argues that it is safe for dogs to surf. What are the reasons? The reasons or premises are that there are people in the water to make sure the dogs are safe, many of the dogs wear doggie life jackets, and no dog has ever drowned.

Rick's argument: Conclusion: Dogs shouldn't be allowed to go surfing.
P1: Surfing isn't safe.
P2: The dogs are being forced to do something they don't want to do.
P3: The owners are taking risks with their dogs.
P4: It is wrong to dress dogs in costumes.
P5: The dogs are being used by their owners.

Stacy's argument: Conclusion: Dogs should be allowed to go surfing.
P1: It is safe.
P2: The dogs are having fun.
P3: The competition raises money to help animal welfare organizations.
P4: The competition brings money that is needed into the community.
P5: Owners aren't putting their dogs at risk.
P6: The competition is fun for everyone.

5. **Surfing Goats** (p. 185)
Rick's argument
Type of argument: argument from authority.
Reasons: Rick claims that his aunt is an expert on goats (after all she has raised goats for over 20 years); so he argues that if she says they hate getting wet, then they do hate getting wet. This type of argument concludes something is true because an expert or an eyewitness says it is. In this case, it is Rick's aunt who is the expert—on goats.
Conclusion: Goats hate getting wet.

Lakeisha's argument

Type of argument: inductive generalization.

Reasons: Lakeisha argues that because these two goats go into the water and have fun surfing, then other goats probably go into the water and have fun surfing too. In this type of argument the conclusion about a group is based on a sample, so it is argued that because a sample has a certain characteristic, then the group does too. Note: If it is appropriate to the discussion ask the students if they think two goats are a large enough sample from which to draw a conclusion. It isn't—and because of this Lakeisha commits a fallacy called a hasty generalization, which we will examine in the next chapter.

Conclusion: Other goats probably get into the water and have fun surfing too.

Tyler's argument

Type of argument: argument from analogy.

Reasons: Tyler's argument is based on a similarity (an analogy) between dogs and goats. So if the dogs have certain attributes, then the goats do too. In this case, the dogs that surf aren't afraid of the water or they wouldn't get in it, they don't mind surfboards or they wouldn't be on them, and they like to surf. So the similarities are that the goats that surf aren't afraid of the water or they wouldn't get in it, and they also don't mind surfboards or they wouldn't be on them.

Conclusion: The goats like to surf too.

Note regarding arguments from analogy: Basic arguments from analogy have the structure seen in this argument, which is:

Entity A has attributes a, b, c, and z.

Entity B has attributes a, b, c.

Therefore, entity B probably has attribute z also.[3]

In Tyler's argument entity A = dogs that surf, and entity B = goats that surf.   The attributes are: a = aren't afraid of the water or they wouldn't be in it, b = don't mind surf boards or they wouldn't be on them, and z = like to surf.

---

3. This structure is from Patrick J. Hurley, *A Concise Introduction to Logic* (Instructor's Edition), 9th ed., (Wadsworth: 2006), 452.

Chapter 6
Informal Fallacies

6.1   (pages 186-187)

Student Poll (p. 186): Answers will vary. This activity has students evaluate the reasoning of the argument, which is reflected in their rating scores. The goal of the activity is that, while they may not be able to identify the problem in the argument, students can see that something is wrong with the reasoning of the argument. They will run into this argument again in section 6.4 when they learn about the fallacy called false cause.

The "Why Should I Care?" Thought Experiment (p. 187): Answers will vary. Students need to explain why it is important to care about fallacies and provide an example that shows what can happen when we don't care about them. This activity will require them to use a number of the cognitive skills essential to critical thinking, such as comprehension, evaluation, construction, and communication. Critical thinkers should care about fallacies because they want to avoid committing errors in their reasoning and because the want to avoid being taken in by the errors in reasoning that other people make intentionally or not. If people don't care about fallacies, then they may get taken in, for example, by arguments that have no evidence but hook their emotions, such as seen in some ads that want money to help victims but provide no evidence that that the money will really help the victims, or by people who use pity instead of evidence as the reason for buying into their argument. Caring about fallacies means learning about different types of fallacies, why they can be so persuasive, and in what ways they fail in reasoning.

6.2   (pages 188-199)

My Prediction (p. 188): Predictions will vary. Students are asked to make a prediction about the young man in the metro with the green surfboard. Since they are learning about fallacies, the goal is for them to make some connection back to poor reasoning in a argument. While they may have no idea about the superstition associated with wearing green or using a green board in the ocean, they should be able to connect the superstition in the argument with poor reasoning and/or fallacies.

Student Poll (p. 190): The students must evaluate the argument in terms of whether or not it commits the fallacy appeal to force. This poll measures the comprehension of the students regarding the fallacy appeal to force and has them evaluate an argument in terms of it. The argument does not commit the fallacy appeal to force because the argument provides specific reasons that support the conclusion that Syria must not move or use their chemical or biological weapons. This means that the threat of force in this instance is relevant to the conclusion.

Argument from Compassion Thought Experiment (p. 193): Answers will vary. Students are testing their comprehension about this type of argument and then constructing their own argument. These will be used later in activity #2 in 6.9 Group Activities & Discussion.

Student Poll (p. 194): Answers will vary. Students are asked to analyze the arguments in terms of how persuasive they are. This has them consider how they might get swept up emotionally and, as a consequence, fail to look for evidence that supports the conclusion. This poll can be a discussion starter in small groups or a large group. It will bring in a discussion about the evidence, the use of emotion, how they were or were not hooked by emotion, and if they failed to look for and demand evidence.

The Considering Someone's Circumstances Thought Experiment (p. 196): Students are asked to consider if it is ever appropriate to consider someone's circumstances as a way to refute an argument. They must also explain their answer. The answer to this question is "yes" but with a qualified "yes." If an arguer has a vested interest in an issue, a candidate, or a situation, then it is important for students to look closely at the argument being made, especially the evidence. They should not simply accept it. At the same time, they should not dismiss an argument just because the other person has a vested interested in the argument; instead, they need to evaluate the argument. In addition, there are times when a person's character matters, such as when we are dealing with a witness or someone giving a testimonial.

Fallacies of Relevance Practice   (p. 198)

1. Fallacy committed; Appeal to pity; The arguer describes the pitiful circumstances of Sallie and offers these circumstances as evidence as to why she should be promoted to the position of supervisor. This is not an argument from compassion. No genuine evidence is offered as to why Sallie deserves to be promoted.

2. No fallacy.

3. Fallacy committed; *Ad hominem*; The arguer attacks Warren Buffet by saying he suffers from dementia and calls his argument for increasing the tax rates for high-income taxpayers "crazy ramblings."

4. No fallacy.

5. Fallacy committed; Appeal to force; The arguer is threatening the loss of jobs for the part-time instructors who support forming a union. The threat is offered as the reason for the conclusion that part-time instructors should not form a union. Students should notice that sometimes the conclusion (and even the premises) can be implied and not directly stated. It is always important to first identify the conclusion and then identify the premises before any evaluation of an argument occurs.

6.3   (pages 200-208)

Student Poll (p. 200): Answers will vary. Students are to evaluate the quality of the evidence provided in the argument. This forces them to examine the argument to see if the evidence provides support for the conclusion. They will also have to explain their own reasoning behind their rating choice. By doing this, the students will work on developing their communication skills.

Missing Premise (p. 201): Active euthanasia is murder.

Student Poll (p. 203): Answers will vary. This student poll functions like a preassessment for the students, and it primes them for the discussion about the fallacy of false dichotomy. The students will have the opportunity to take a closer look at the two examples after the fallacy is introduced. This will allow them to think about their answers as they learn about the fallacy and perhaps have some of their own "aha!" moments before the examples are discussed.

John's Disjunctive Argument   (p. 205)

Conclusion: You will buy me a new car to drive to school.
Missing premise: I know you don't want me to drive this old death trap that is dangerous and could get me killed.

Driving the Old Death Trap Thought Experiment (p. 205): Some alternatives are that John could take the school bus or a city bus to school, or his car could be repaired, or his parents could buy him a used car.

Prediction Revision (p. 205): Now that students are introduced to the topic, they can consider whether they want to revise their prediction or not.

Fallacies of Presumption Practice (p. 207)

1. No fallacy. This is an argument from definition, a deductive argument form covered in Section 5.4. The conclusion depends upon the definition of the word "bachelor."

2. Fallacy committed; false dichotomy. The arguer has set up the argument as if there are only two possible alternatives: either their next truck will be a Ford F-150 4WD or they will go bankrupt paying for gasoline. They could buy another model or brand of car that gets good gas mileage. The Ford F-150 4WD isn't the only car that is capable of getting good gas mileage. Because there are other possible alternatives, the argument commits the fallacy.

3. Fallacy committed; false dichotomy. Both the premise and conclusion are missing. The missing premise is: I'm sure you don't want to never go on another vacation (double negation) OR I'm sure you want to go on other vacations. The missing conclusion is: So you will take a smaller suitcase.

4. Fallacy committed; Begging the question, the circular version.

5. No fallacy.

6. No fallacy.

6.4   (pages 209-218)

Student Poll (p. 210): Answers will vary. Students are asked to evaluate the trustworthiness of the authorities in the two examples, and then explain their rationale. The point of this exercise is to enable them to learn how to evaluate someone who is presented as an authority, identifying those who are qualified authorities from those who are not. This is critical to being able to detect the fallacy of unqualified authority.

The Surf Board Thought Experiment (pp. 211-212): Answers will vary. Students are to explain whether or not they are convinced by his argument. This forces the students to evaluate the argument and primes students for the discussion of false cause that follows. In thinking of a response to the argument, students must decide how to communicate their position.

Student Poll (p. 213): Answers will vary. The students rate the son's argument and then reflect on whether or not they have encountered false cause before in their own life experience or committed this argument themselves. It also has them evaluate why people might commit this fallacy and whether or not it actually affects their results. This makes learning about fallacies relevant to their life.

Student Poll (p. 214): Answers will vary. This poll has the students evaluate why the grade level at which children read has declined. By finding additional factors that have affected why children read at a lower level, it shows them that Example 4 commits the oversimplified cause fallacy, one kind of false cause.

Fallacies of Weak Induction Practice (p. 217)

1. Appeal to unqualified authority; Beyoncé is not an expert on car safety; therefore, she is not able to recommend a car as the best car to buy based on safety issues.

2. False cause (temporal succession); The argument's conclusion rests on the premise that watching

television causes the arguer to have to do chores. This is due to temporal succession—first the arguer watches television, and then the arguer has to do chores.

3. Hasty generalization; The conclusion is based on too small of a sample—only one mistake is cited as the evidence for the conclusion.

4. No fallacy.

5. Hasty generalization; The sample is too small; it is based on only one day of class.

6. False cause (oversimplified cause); While getting notoriety and instant gratification on social media is one cause for the increase in vandalism in U.S. National Parks, there are other reasons for the vandalism, including the encroachment of urban areas on the National Parks, lack of moral boundaries by the offenders, inflated self-worth and sense of entitlement, a thrill seeking trend, and lack of parental control.

6.5   (pages 219-226)

Student Poll (p. 219): All four of the arguments commit the fallacy of equivocation.

Argument 1 equivocates "man"—human being and male.
Argument 2 equivocates "wicked"—very good and dangerous.
Argument 3 equivocates the relative pronoun "large"; what is "large" depends upon the context.
Argument 4 equivocates "public interest"—what the public is interested in and the public welfare.

Amphiboly Thought Experiment   (pp. 221-223)

Example 1: The problem is due to the way the sign is written. Interpretations: (1) The pronoun "your" refers to the lions in the car, so they are told to stay in the car. (2) The "your" refers to humans who are driving in the vicinity, so due to lions in the area, the humans are to remain in their cars.

Example 2: The problem is due to how we read the headline. Interpretations: (1) To try shooting the defendant. (2) To try the shooting defendant.

Example 3: The problem is due to the way the contract is written. Fred Sally's interpretation: He is entitled to the money because he finished the job but not the pool table because he missed the deadline. Barbara Sikes's interpretation: Her nephew Fred Sally is not entitled to the money for the job or the pool table because he did not finish the work by the deadline.

Fallacies of Ambiguity Practice   (p. 225)

1. Amphiboly; The problem is a misplaced modifier ("at the request of her husband").

2. No fallacy.

3. Equivocation; The word that is equivocated is "right" as in "a good thing to do" and "something to which someone has a claim."

4. Equivocation; What is equivocated is 40%. The 40% applies only to the plane ticket.

5. No fallacy.

6. Amphiboly; The problem is a dangling phrase. The sentence suggests that the lawyer is the one who has been declared mentally incompetent.

6.6   (pages 227-234)

Check-in (p. 227): This chapter may be difficult for some students, so it is important that all students do the self-assessments. Any students selecting the baboon need to seek coaching from another student or the teacher.

The "Why Commit Fallacies?" Thought Experiment (p. 227): Answers will vary. This Thought Experiment has students identify several reasons why people might commit fallacies. This will help them understand why they, too, might commit fallacies.

Student Poll (p. 228): Answers will vary. Students evaluate which of the fallacies might be persuasive and trip them up. To do this, they will have to think about each of the fallacies and how they might be hooked by them. This would be useful as the basis of a class discussion because it would help students understand that everyone has to look out for fallacies, and it would lead to a good review about the fallacies in this chapter.

The Fallacies Quiz (pp. 229-230): Their score will provide them with feedback about how well they understand the material and mastered it. It will help them identify if and where they need further help.

1. b
2. c
3. b
4. a
5. a
6. b
7. c
8. c
9. b
10. a

6.7   (pages 235-237)

Important Takeaways (p. 237): The students need to think about how informal fallacies matter to their personal life. This will help them identify three important takeaways from this chapter that they wish to remember. The point of this activity is to have students learn to make direct connections between the content of this course and their own lives. If they do, then they will have a much better chance of applying what they've learned about critical thinking and, by doing so, grow as a critical thinker.

6.8   (pages 238-241)

Fallacy Inspection

1. Fallacy; amphiboly; The problem is a misplaced modifier ("in my pajamas").

2. Fallacy; false cause; The kind of false cause is *post hoc ergo proper hoc*. This mistake focuses around temporal succession, or one event coming before another event. Temporal succession isn't enough to create a causal connection.

3. Fallacy; amphiboly; The problem is a dangling participial phrase. What is implied is that the detective was in the coma.

4. Fallacy; appeal to force; There is a threat of harm: John will lose his job (be fired) if he doesn't cut the budget by $25,000.

5. Fallacy; begging the question; The premise restates the conclusion.

6. Fallacy; hasty generalization; The sample is too small—one movie written by Spielberg that is terrible

does not constitute a large enough sample to draw a conclusion.

7. Fallacy; false dichotomy; Notice the argument, which only provides the "either … or …" premise and leaves out the second premise and conclusion, offers two alternatives as if they are the only ones possible: build a park or build a storage facility for nuclear waste. Are these really the only alternatives? This is a good example of how someone who wants a certain choice selected (build a park) sets up the choices so that the desired choice will be selected because there is no way anyone would prefer the alternative choice (build a storage facility for nuclear waste).

8. No fallacy.

9. Fallacy; appeal to pity; The speaker provides a long litany of sad things that have nothing to do with whether he/she has earned all the points for the essay on the exam.

10. Fallacy; false cause; This is an example of the kind of false cause called oversimplified cause. If it is true that the quality of education is our high schools has been getting worse for years, then it is due to a confluence of a number of reasons, one of which is that the reading level in textbooks gets lower every year. However, additional reasons exist, such as some schools gear teaching to test results, lack of support and involvement by parents in their children's learning, lack of books and other educational resources for children in many schools (e.g., in some schools there are not enough books for each child in the class), overcrowded classrooms, budget cuts to education, and the effects of poverty and homelessness on children at school.

11. Fallacy; begging the question; This is an example of circular reasoning.

12. No fallacy.

6.9   (pages 242-244)

The Fallacy Bowl (p. 242): see answers for 6.8 The Fallacy Inspection.

Appeal to Pity or Argument From Compassion (p. 242): The answers will depend upon the arguments that the students write. The teacher needs to visit each group to provide some feedback about their arguments.

The Fallacy Scavenger Hunt (pp. 243-244)

1. Definition of a fallacy is found on page 186, and the definition of a fallacy is that it is a flaw in an argument that is due to something other than simply having false premises.

2. In *ad hominem* abusive, the arguer responds to the other person's argument by verbally abusing and attacking the other person, either crudely or subtly. However, in *ad hominem* circumstantial, the arguer does not resort to verbal abuse or name-calling in order to discredit the opponent's argument, but instead, the arguer does so by alluding to specific circumstances that affect the opponent.

3. In appeal to pity the arguer attempts to get the conclusion to the argument accepted by evoking pity from the listener or reader and not by providing genuine evidence for the conclusion. An argument from compassion is not a fallacy. It is an argument that evokes compassion on behalf of someone, a group, or even animals. This type of argument provides genuine reasons or evidence as to why special consideration is deserved; for example, that the person is a true victim of circumstances and that the special consideration will really help the person, such as in the appeals by the Red Cross during hurricane Katrina.

4. The explanation of a false dichotomy is found on page 204. It is an argument in which one of the

premises provides an "either ... or ..." statement that hides additional alternatives. In other words, it presents the two options as if they are the only two possible choices, one of which is clearly unacceptable, in an attempt to get another person or group to accept the alternative the arguer is pushing for. The arguer is trying to trick the listener or reader by creating the illusion that there are no other possible alternatives.

5. In false cause the problem is that the causal connection which the arguer believes exists between cause and effect does not actually exist or at the very least is highly questionable. We often get hooked because there is a correlation between the two events; however, a correlation does not necessarily mean that one event is the cause of the other.

6. An example of false cause is an athlete who attributes her success in making every basket she attempts in a basketball game to following a ritual before the game or to wearing the same dirty socks every game. Another example is arguing that video games are solely responsible for the decline in the reading level of children. The problem here is a type of false cause that is due to oversimplification.

7. In hasty generalization the conclusion is drawn from a sample that is either two small or atypical. An example of this is found in stereotypes or in racial or religious prejudice. Another example is arguing that pit bull dogs and pit bull dog mixes are dangerous and need to be banned based solely on a few very highly publicized incidents.

8. Both equivocation and amphiboly deal with ambiguity; however, in equivocation the ambiguity is due to the double meaning of a word. The premise will imply one meaning, but the conclusion will be based on another. In amphiboly, the ambiguity is due to a grammatical or punctuation error or how the words are arranged.

9. The explanation for appeal to force is found on page 189. The fallacy of appeal to force involves a threat of physical or psychological harm if the conclusion is not accepted. The threat of harm substitutes for any real evidence that would support the conclusion.

10. Critical thinkers should care about fallacies because they want to avoid committing errors in their reasoning, and they want to avoid being taken in by the errors in reasoning that other people make intentionally or not. Also, some fallacies can be very persuasive, so if we don't understand them or how to detect them, then we will be fooled by them and may even make some of these same errors in our own arguments.

11. Gladys' five suggestions for detecting and avoiding fallacies are: (1) Pay close attention to the argument, looking closely at the conclusion, the premises, and the meaning of these. (2) Check to see that the evidence (the premises) supports the conclusion of the argument. (3) Be cautious when arguments use emotionally charged language because it is easy to get caught up in the emotion and accept the value claim without demanding evidence to support the conclusion. (4) Be aware of your own worldview because it can impact your creation and evaluation of arguments. (5) Trust your instinct if an argument seems questionable. Never buy into an argument if it seems questionable to you. Take the time to look carefully at it and evaluate it.

12. Answers will vary depending on who is a Fallacy Master. If there are none in the class, then the answer is "None in the class."

13. Answers will vary depending on who is a Fallacy Knight. If there are none in the class, then the answer is "None in the class."

14. The sticker is given out once the pair of students shows the teacher that they have completed questions 1-13.

Chapter 7
Advertising

7.1   (pages 245-248)

The "All-Time Best Ever" Thought Experiment (p. 245): Answers will vary. Students are asked to identify their favorite and least favorite commercials and explain why. This gets students to consider what techniques are used in commercials that grab their attention and why commercials might fail.

Student Poll (p. 246): Answers will vary. In the first poll, students are to identify all the places where they encounter advertising. This helps them realize how pervasive advertising is without them even realizing it.

Student Poll (p. 246): Answers will vary. In the second poll, students are asked to rate whether they think advertising is out of control, and if so, then how much. This poll has them consider their feelings about the pervasiveness of advertising.

Student Poll (p. 247): Answers will vary. In the third poll, students must identify who they think the top four advertisers are in the United States, how much money is spent in advertising, and what country spends the most. In order to identify who they believe are the top four advertisers, students will need to reflect on their own exposure to advertising—what companies' advertising they notice the most. It would be interesting to compare answers in class to see if the students are noticing the same companies. This could be tied to who is targeting teens.

7.2   (pages 249-272)

Explaining to Aliens Thought Experiment (p. 249): Answers will vary. This Thought Experiment asks students to evaluate the value of advertising and whether there are any benefits associated with it or not. This primes the students for the discussion that will follow in this section on the benefits and criticism of advertising.

Student Poll (p. 249): Answers will vary. Students are asked to wrestle with advertising's relationship to them and to society. This would also be a useful Student Poll to share in a large group. It would generate a productive discussion around their relationship to advertising and get them to begin thinking about how advertising affects them.

Texting and Driving Prevention PSAs Thought Experiment (pp. 251-252): This Thought Experiment makes use of two PSA commercials on texting and driving: "On My Way" (the 30 second one) and "5 Seconds"—both of which can be found on YouTube.

1. The target audience is a teen audience.

2. Do not text and drive—it is dangerous and you could die—someone you care about could die.

3. 5 seconds

4. Students decide for themselves whether the message was clear in the two PSAs. If they don't think they are clear, then you might ask them what would make the message even clearer.

5. Students decide which PSA impacted them the most.

6. Students must explain why the PSA that they chose had the greatest impact on them.

7. Students must reflect on the value of these PSAs in terms of impact—would they really prevent their friends and classmates from texting and driving. They are also required to provide their reasoning.

8. Students must evaluate the two PSAs in terms of audience. If the target audience for the PSAs is a teen audience, then would this be as effective with an older audience? If not, then what would make the PSAs effective? Actually, they are quite effective even though the characters are teens. Adults can relate to running late and feeling the need to let friends know that they are on their way or to having a text come in and feeling the need to see what it says. Plus, both PSAs have a shock value. Perhaps having a PSA with an adult driving would make it even better if adults are the target audience.

9. Students are asked to evaluate a PSA print ad as to its effectiveness with teens. This requires them to analyze and evaluate what they think makes a print ad successful—and particularly with their age group. It also has them evaluate the ad and its techniques.

10. Students are asked compare a print ad with a commercial—and specifically the one print ad they were provided. This helps them consider the "why" behind their choice of which medium impacts them the most.

My Prediction (p. 254): Predictions will vary. The students are asked to respond to a Milky Way ad that appeared during the Olympics. It will require students to use the skills of analysis and evaluation as they consider the ad. The prediction activity is priming the students for the discussion on the various techniques used in advertising. If they find the ad funny, then they will have experienced the success of one of the key techniques used in the ad.

Student Poll (p. 255): Answers will vary. In this poll, students are asked to evaluate the list of criticisms regarding advertising that this section will look at. Then they are to prioritize them according to their importance. If they don't agree with one, then they have the option to give it a zero, or they can even add one of their own and rank it.

"What's It Telling Me?" Thought Experiment (pp. 257-259)

Alcoa ad (pp. 257-258)

1. the Alcoa HyTop Closure—a bottle cap

2. Women are the target audience. The ad is woman to woman. The woman in the ad is looking at the women reading the ad and letting then know that she can open the bottle without assistance. The picture and the copy immediately under the picture with "woman" underlined drives home who the target is.

3. The woman is looking at us, and she has a surprised and even amazed look (her eyes and mouth give that away) that she can open the bottle.

4. The copy tells us that women either have a common experience of not being strong enough to open bottles without a man's help or they are perceived that way. This ad is emphasizing the ease of opening the bottle due to this new type of bottle cap—the Alcoa HyTop Closure—a product that would appeal to women if they typically have problems opening bottles. The copy is marketing the cap to women, who do most of the grocery shopping as single women and married women, and it is trying to influence

them to buy the products that make use of this bottle cap.

5. It tells us that (1) women do most of the grocery shopping in the culture and in this regard make monetary decisions that the company wants to tap into, (2) that women are not perceived as physically strong—they typically need men to open bottles for them, and this bottle cap does not require "muscle power," (3) women are perceived as "dainty," and (4) the modern woman appreciates some sense of independence—after all, the product will enable a woman to easily open bottles without the help of a man—even a husband.

6. Students must evaluate the ad and relate it to their own culture and how gender roles have changed (or not) in order to decide if this is a good ad for today. Their answer needs to demonstrate that they have thought about the culture in the ad and their own culture and how they are similar or different.

Van Heusen ad   (pp. 258-259)

1. Ties

2. He is in charge—a king of his domain—and feels superior. He feels entitled to be waited upon by the woman in the ad. He doesn't even look at the woman, who is looking up at him. He is fully dressed, but she is not—she wears her robe. The image tells us that men and women were not considered equal at the time the ad was made. The copy makes clear that the world belongs to men. It is not an accident that the word "power" is related to the word "man." The command to "Show her it's a man's world" is reflected in how the man in the bed is relating to the woman. There is also the belief of this period that women are "happy" that it is a "man's world." This reinforces the gender roles that appear in the ad.

3. The woman is subservient. She is on her knees in a supplicant position offering up the breakfast to her master. Note she does not eat with him. This is a traditional position that we see from history of supplicants and how those without power approach those who rule. The woman also looks like she wants to please the man and is looking for a sign that he is pleased—though he looks off into space away from her. She is also made vulnerable by being undressed. This tells us that the culture at the time did not consider women to be men's equals, that a woman's job was to take care of a man's needs and see that he was happy, and that women did not have the power that men did.

4. The man is dressed in shirt and tie and the woman is dressed in her robe. The man is lying in bed with his hands behind his head looking away. The body position is one of power and entitlement as he dismisses or ignores the woman serving him. She is on her knees before him serving him his breakfast.

5. They are not equally powerful. The position, actions, dress, and copy make clear that the man is superior and powerful while the woman is not.

6. The copy tells us that the tie is a symbol of the man's power and communicates to the woman that he is the boss and she is subservient. It also tells us that both parties know this and that she is happy about it. This being "happy" is there in the copy to reinforce the gender roles and to validate these roles. After all, what could be wrong with them if she is happy? She likes that it is a man's world and that she gets to wait on him. Her hope is that he will notice her and be pleased.

7. Students must evaluate the ad and relate it to their own culture and how gender roles have changed (or not) in order to decide if this is a good ad for today. Their answer needs to demonstrate that they have thought about the culture in the ad and their own culture and how they are similar or different.

Males in Advertising Thought Experiment (pp. 260-262)

Dockers ad   (p. 261)

1. The ad implies that men—not women—are the ones who should wear the pants. This is not about physically wearing pants but about who is in control and in charge—who has the power. Men need to behave "like a man" and not be emasculated. Notice the posture of the man—the body language of the man—wide stance and the crossed arms—shows that he is in charge and not to be messed with. Also note that Dockers are the pants to wear if you are that powerful man.

2. It says that men are in charge and have the power—not women

3. Students need to consider the culture's gender roles today as well as the population at their school in order to answer this question.

Corona Extra Beer ad   (pp. 261-262)

1. The target audience is the teen male, especially one who is athletic. The ad shows a group of soccer players on the left and a male on the right dragging some heavy, huge baggage from his youth when he was a ballet dancer.

2. Real men don't dance ballet. Notice the stance of the group of males. Notice how the lone male is struggling with his load. Who would want to be a ballet dancer? It is seen as effeminate and not what real men do. In actuality, ballet dancers are supreme athletes—very strong, fit, flexible, and coordinated. NFL players are encouraged to take ballet to strengthen their calf and thigh muscles. Wide receiver and Hall of Famer Lynn Swan, for example, had taken ballet to prepare for his game, Steelers nose tackle Steve McLendon has also taken ballet, and the University of Memphis requires that their football players take ballet and yoga for flexibility and agility. This ad primes the students for the discussion that follows on ads and stereotypes.

Student Poll (p. 263): Answers will vary. Students are asked to respond from their perspective as to whether or not advertising can be used to fight stereotypes and whether or not they have ever seen ads that show women as liberated and independent and males as capable of doing household chores or as loving and caring.

Student Poll (pp. 264-265): Answers will vary. Students are to rate the ads for how well they think the ads fight stereotypes. The ads are: (1) AT&T/Bell Phone Co, (2) Ariel Laundry Soap, (3) Noxzema, and (4) Lego. This would lend itself to a large group discussion on how students rated the ads and why.

Student Poll (p. 266): Answers will vary. This poll looks at the spending power of children and teens. It is priming them for the discussion about why advertisers are so interested in marketing to children and teens.

"What Should a Psychologist Do?" Thought Experiment (p. 268): Answers will vary. Students are asked to articulate their position regarding whether or not it is right for companies to use psychological theories, psychological research, and/or psychologists in order to sell their products to children. This requires students to utilize a number of their critical thinking skills, such as comprehension, analysis, evaluation, and communication. Their answer should demonstrate that they have thought carefully about what they've learned and then constructed a position. This would be an excellent topic to discuss in class or for a debate.

The "Who is to Blame?" Thought Experiment (p. 269): Answers will vary. Students are asked to respond to the question on the cover of the Sports Illustrated magazine: "Sneakers and team jackets are hot, sometimes too hot. Kids are being mugged, even killed for them. Who's at fault?" The topic is complicated, and students should be helped to not oversimplify the cause. Some of the causes are these:

- Companies create artificial shortages for popular products.
- Companies use advertising (and celebrity endorsements) to create status around owning/wearing certain products and thus create the desire for the products.
- Companies set a high price for status products.
- Culture as a whole is materialistic and values status and status brands, which reinforces that human worth is tied to owning/wearing certain products.
- Children from economically challenged families do not have the resources to buy the status products.
- Some families are not helping their children to develop moral values and self-worth that are not tied to materialism and status. This, too, must not be oversimplified as families need support within their culture to do this, such as from schools and churches. Children need an alternative narrative to buy into. This can be a challenge for families given the power of a culture that ties status and self-worth to materialism.
- Consumerism itself plays a role in this.
- Peer pressure is also part of the problem.

This Thought Experiment would be very suited to a large group discussion. It is important for students to learn that often issues are quite complex and need to be looked at from a number of perspectives. This helps them grow as critical thinkers.

Student Poll (p. 270): Answers will vary. This poll has students do some critical thinking around the use of sex and violence to sell products. This is an important topic to discuss in the classroom because students encounter sex and violence in print ads, online ads, outdoor ads, and in commercials. They need help in understanding how sex and violence are being used and how it affects them; however, there needs to be some sensitivity in its treatment given the age level of the students and parental concerns. We have chosen not to show many of the typical ads that students see because some parents may be uncomfortable with this. One suggestion is to have students bring in examples of ads they find in their own magazines and use those for a discussion. To ignore this topic does not help students comprehend what the ads are doing or help them learn how to evaluate them. If students are going to be good critical thinkers, then the topic of sex and violence in advertising needs to be addressed since sex is one of the leading advertising techniques.

Student Poll (p. 272): Answers will vary. This poll takes another look at the students' relationship to advertising. Students are asked to evaluate how susceptible they are to advertising as well as how susceptible the adults in their families, their closest friends, and teens in general are to advertising. This leads them in particular to own how advertising affects them and begins priming them for the discussion at the end of the chapter about how to resist the persuasive techniques used by advertising.

7.3   (pages 273-276)

What Ads Do Quiz   (p. 276)

1. Milk – particularly low-fat or fat-free milk
2. Buy and drink milk.

3. Identification advertisement

4. The ad wants teens to identify with Taylor Swift, and it also makes a promise that if the teens drink milk, they will be leaner and build muscle. This promise is indirect—notice how "Taylor" mentions that "some studies suggest" that by skipping soda ("sugary drinks") and drinking milk teens will "tend to be" leaner.

7.4   (pages 277-280)

Student Poll (p. 279): Answers will vary. Students are asked to rate how they feel about the fact that advertisers can create brand equity without them being aware of it. This poll personalizes the topic for students and reinforces buy-in regarding the topic.

7.5   (pages 281-314)

Transfer Practice I (p. 282)

1. The image conveys speed, power. The students answers will vary about the feelings the image produces in them, but some possible answers are: positive feelings of being powerful, strong, I can be a winner like this fast jaguar.

2. The words that stand out: "speed," "Ask the master." Answer will vary as to what the students might desire, but some possible answers are: Make me want to be fast like this jaguar—want shoes that will help me go—be a winner. It is not an accident that the words "Ask the master" is on the same line as the Nike logo. These words do not only apply to the jaguar. The inference is that the master of speed, the one with the secret, is Nike.

3. The ad associates positive regard with the brand, being a winner, being "the master"—the one with the secret on how to have speed and be powerful.

4. Students are asked to evaluate the ad and communicate their reason for why the ad is successful or not.

Transfer Practice II (p. 283)

1. The images that are used: flowers; a soft-looking, stuffed bear; color purple. The feelings that these generate are overall positive. The light purple color creates an up, happy feeling. The picture of the flowers also adds to the positive feeling of the product. The bear looks soft and cuddly and is doing a happy act of dancing and releasing flowers. Teddy bears are generally perceived in a positive way; they are often associated with affection since many people had teddy bears as children.

2. The name of the product is "Snuggle," which conveys a positive feeling. The bear is cuddly-looking and reinforces the name of the product—"Snuggle." The word "exhilarations" also transfers positive feelings to the product. The sans serif font, used in the name of the product, creates a fun, friendly, approachable feeling. The psychology of fonts is very interesting. A study was done by Wichita State University to "determine if certain personalities and uses are associated with various fonts."[4] Fonts like Comic Sans, which is similar to the font used in the ad—this is Comic Sans: Snuggle—is perceived as cuddly, youthful, and happy. The selection of the font in this ad is not an accident, and it is slected to help create positive feelings that will transfer to the brand and create positive brand equity.

3. The images and words create positive, happy feelings in the consumer and the advertiser wants that transferred to the brand.

4. A. Dawn Shaikh, Barbara S. Chaparro, and Doug Fox, "Perception of Fonts: Perceived Personality Traits and Uses," *Usability News*, Vol. 8 Issue 1, Febrauary 2006, http://psychology.wichita.edu/surl/usabilitynews/81/PersonalityofFonts.asp.

4. Students need to evaluate the ad in terms of how well it transfers positive feelings to the brand. They also need to provide some rationale for their answer.

Student Poll – Technique Humor (p. 289): Answers will vary. Students need to evaluate the ads and the commercial in terms of how funny they are. This poll helps to personalize the lesson and get them actively involved in it. It is important that students are not simply passive viewers of the advertising but are involved in applying their critical thinking skills.

Student Poll – Technique Celebrity Endorsement (p. 294): Answers will vary. Students are asked to evaluate the impact that celebrity endorsements have on them. This is important as critical thinkers viewing advertising. We need to know how we are affected by these various techniques so that we can prevent ourselves from falling prey to them and being persuaded without our realizing it.

Student Poll – Weasel Words (p. 296): Answers will vary. Students are to evaluate how susceptible they are to the weasel words found in the ad: "Summer Clearance Sale" and "Save Up to 50%." This helps them identify which type of advertising techniques they need to watch out for.

Student Poll – Music (p. 301): Students are to evaluate if they have ever heard music used in the stores where they shop, and if so, how that music has impacted them and their choice to buy merchandise.

Check-In (p. 302): If students are selecting the teen who says "Say what?" then encourage them to seek coaching. These check-ins are student self-assessments that help students monitor when they need coaching. It also motivates them to take personal accountability for their learning.

Advertising Techniques Practice (pp. 303-314)

1. transfer; sex; celebrity endorsement

2. transfer; humor; slogan, tagline; logo

3. humor; emotional appeal (fear); slogan, tagline; logo

4. transfer; puffery; slogan, tagline

5. transfer; emotional appeal (happiness); puffery; sex; slogan, tagline; logo

6. transfer; bandwagon; emotional appeal (happiness); logo

7. transfer; emotional appeal (happiness, altruism); slogan, tagline; logo

8. bandwagon; slogan, tagline; logo

9. transfer; bandwagon; emotional appeal (sexy, desired); puffery; sex; slogan, tagline; celebrity endorsement

10. transfer; bandwagon; emotional appeal (to be outstanding, to go for it); slogan, tagline; logo

11. transfer; humor; slogan, tagline; logo

12. transfer; slogan, tagline; celebrity endorsement; logo

13. "Become a Hero" (p. 309)
    a. To become a hero you need to buy one of the specially marked bags of PEDIGREE® Food that

has a hero coupon inside the bag. When you buy something else using one of the coupons, then PEDIGREE® matches the value with a donation to PetSmart Charities. You are a hero when the donation is made to PetSmart Charities by PEDIGREE®.

b. To redeem a coupon, you have to purchase a product represented by the coupon.

c. All three: money is given to PetSmart Charities, PEDIGREE® makes money, and you get both the product you bought and the satisfaction that some money (no matter how small) was donated to PetSmart Charities.

d. Students must evaluate whether or not this ad is a good one and provide their rationale.

14. "Campbell's Soup" (pp. 310-311)

a. Students need to identify how the image of the boy and the dad eating their soup together makes them feel. Expect answers such as: happy, hungry, nostalgic, positive.

b. The dominant colors in the ad are red and white—like the Campbell's soup can.

c. These colors were chosen because (1) they reinforce the brand, (2) they make the soup look appealing, (3) the picture is striking visually, and (4) the color red is a dynamic color that is exciting and associated with warmth, life, passion, strength, and excitement, (5) the color red can also stimulate the appetite (this is why red is often used in restaurants), and (6) research has found that people find red-colored food to be the most appealing. In this picture the red is a warm red that creates a cozy, warm, intimate feeling.

d. The word "good" appears 10 times in the ad.

e. Things that are "good" are positive and we want them in our life, so the ad is trying to get the word "good" associated with the brand and to transfer these positive feelings to the brand.

f. Some of the good things that happen when you eat soup: you share the soup with the people you like; you feel good "all over"; you enjoy the taste; you want to eat; you enjoy the meal; you eat nutritious food that is full of protein, minerals, and vitamins; you warm up; and you calm down.

g. Students are asked to reflect on how the copy "to warm you up … to gentle you down … to make you feel good all over …" makes them feel. This points to the the emotional appeal of the ad and to what feeling the ad wants to transfer to the brand.

h. Students must evaluate the success of the ad (do you want to try Campbell's soup?) and explain their rationale.

i. Students must rate the ad's effectiveness on a scale from 1 to 10. This is another approach to evaluating the success of the ad.

15. "The Mini automatic" (pp. 312-313)

a. Students may have various answers about what they think the woman in the ad is feeling, such as scared, overwhelmed, or confused.

b. Student answers may vary about what the ad is trying to say based on the image and copy, but their answers need to be along the line of: the car makes driving simple enough for a woman; anyone, even a woman, can drive the Mini automatic; because this car is automatic it is an easy car to drive; driving a Mini automatic takes the fear out of driving.

c. Student answers will vary, such as the Mini automatic makes driving easy because you don't have to worry about changing gears, stalling, or grinding into the wrong gear; the Mini automatic makes driving easier and safer. Notice how the copy no longer focuses on gender but, instead, focuses on the car. The image and the copy over the image are to catch people's attention, draw them in, and by using the stereotype of women drivers, underscore the idea of how easy the car is to drive.

    d. Using a Goldie Hawn look-alike is to (1) catch people's attention, (2) transfer the positive feelings people have about Goldie Hawn as well as the positive feeling they have about a humorous ad to the brand, and (3) drive home the idea about the ease of driving the car—so easy that even ditzy people, like Goldie Hawn's character, could drive the car.

    e. Students need to evaluate the ad in terms of how well it would work in today's culture. Their answers will vary; however, they need to provide a rationale to support their "yes" or "no" answer. This focus is not the product per se but the approach of the ad. Some reasons that students might give for a "yes" answer are: it uses humor, or people can relate to how difficult it is to learn to use manual driving, or people want a car that is easy to drive. Some reasons that students might give a "no" answer are: it is considered sexist today to use a stereotype of women as ditzy and bad drivers; automatic cars are common today, so they need to advertise other features of the car; the association of driving and sleeping is problematic for some consumers since deaths on roads due to someone falling asleep at the wheel are common—in fact as of 2005 the National Highway Traffic Safety Administration estimated that 100,000 police-reported accidents are the direct result of people falling asleep at the wheel.

    f. Student are asked to evaluate the effectiveness of the ad.

16. "First for Women Insurance Company Limited" (p. 314)

    a. Based on this ad, the insurance company only covers women because men make poor choices and so are too high a risk.

    b. Students need to answer "Yes" or "No." This isn't the reason that they only cover women. The company was founded to fill a gap in the insurance market. Most financial services companies tailor their products and services to men and not women. First for Women was created to fill that gap and provide the products and services women need. The company does note that statistically "women are lower insurance risks than their male counterparts and the costs to repair a vehicle crashed by a women is on average lower than the cost of damage caused by men." Note: Being a lower insurance risk doesn't mean that this is necessarily due to poor choices or a lack of common sense.

    c. They produced this image and copy to grab people's attention, to use humor to transfer positive feelings to the brand, to get women to jump on the bandwagon, provide an emotional appeal to women, and to get their brand known.

    d. Students need to evaluate whether or not the ad caught their attention.

    e. Students need to evaluate whether or not the ad was successful in terms of getting them to know the brand and remember it.

    f. Students need to identify if they liked the ad or not and provide a rationale for their answer.

7.6   (pages 315-316)

Student Poll (p. 316): Answers will vary. Students are asked to identify their position regarding Photoshopping of images for ads. This Student Poll can be used for discussion as a large group or for a debate.

7.8 (pages 320-323)

Student Poll (p. 321): Answers will vary. Students are asked to rate statements that look at how they view themselves and advertising relative to their use of "Like." This activity is having them stop and consider their use of "Like." As critical thinkers, they need to consider their use of it and how corporations use their "Likes," particularly since data is created from these "Likes" that is stored and used to create their consumer profile. This poll would lend itself to an interesting and lively large group discussion.

Student Poll (p. 322): Answers will vary. This poll has students consider how they participate in marketing without realizing it and how they feel about that.

Student Poll (p. 322): Answers will vary. This poll has students consider how they may have experienced targeted advertising and how they feel about it.

Student Poll (p. 323): Answers will vary. This poll has students decide if it is appropriate for advertisers and corporations to use any technique that works with the teen market and whether or not they feel manipulated by the use of "Like." It might be quite fruitful to have students debate whether advertisers and corporations should be able to use any technique that works on them or whether there are limits that should be set. By this time, students have had a solid, comprehensive look at advertising and should be able to articulate thoughtful positions around this question.

7.9 (pages 324-327)

Important Takeaways (p. 327): Students need to identify three important takeaways about advertising that they want to remember. The chapter has identified many ways that advertising impacts their lives and offered a number of helpful tips about how to be critical viewers of advertising. Students may actually find that selecting only three takeaways is a challenge, but by only selecting three, they will be forced to focus on what is most important to them as they evaluate the content of the chapter in relation to their own lives. A large or small group discussion about their takeaways might be very fruitful. It would encourage discussion of the content, it would facilitate greater buy-in throughout the class, and it would enable students to talk about what they believe is important to them in living their lives as critical thinkers.

7.10 (pages 328-333)

1. **Needs vs. Wants** (p. 328): Answers will vary. Students are asked to consider their own experience of shopping and when they might have impulsively bought something, confusing need vs. want. Then they are to fill out a chart that looks at five things that they are planning to buy or expect to buy soon. The point isn't to make students feel bad about wanting to buy something. The point is to help them tell the difference between their needs and wants, to help them realize that they can be swept up in impulsive decisions to buy, and to help them learn to control their shopping decisions.

2. **Viewing Ads as a Critical Thinker** (pp. 329-330)

   Mountain Dew Ad (p. 329)

   1. Drink Diet Mountain Dew—it is better than before because it has a new taste, which makes it just as tasty as the regular Mountain Dew but minus the calories.

   2. Anyone who drinks diet drinks and Mountain Dew drinkers.

3. Transfer; humor; slogan, tagline; Students may also notice the use of color. The background is the color of Mountain Dew. This also works on us unconsciously to reinforce the identification of the product.

4. Students are asked to evaluate the ad as to whether or not it is successful. They need to provide a thoughtful rationale.

Impaired Driving Ad (p. 330)

1. Don't drink and drive.

2. They drive home that real people died—in this case, young people died. The images of the dead students along with their names help to personalize this plea for people to not drink and drive. The fact that they were athletes is something that also helps us to care about them since we learn more about them. It may also help teens identify with them or for parents or grandparents etc. to think about young people who travel with their teams on trips and might meet up with them if they tend to drink and drive. The copy further emphasizes the personal relationships that people have with those killed by drunk drivers.

3. This ad targets everyone. It obviously targets those who drink, but it also targets nondrinkers, too, by motivating them to intervene when they are with someone who is drinking and will drive or even to encourage those who drink not to drive in the future or to get involved themselves in community campaigns to prevent drinking and driving.

4. Transfer; bandwagon; emotional appeal; logo.

5. Students are asked to evaluate the ad as to how success it is and provide a rationale. This ad might be a great one to discuss in class given the amount of drinking done by teens, who are overrepresented in driving accidents that involve alcohol and in drunk driver injuries and deaths.

3. **Does Advertising Determine Your Tastes?** (p. 331): Answers will vary. Students are asked to evaluate the position of the American Association of Advertising Agencies and then decide if they agree with that position or not. They are also asked to explain their reasoning. This question gets them to reflect on what they have learned about the way that advertisers seek to persuade us to buy their products or use their services. Topics they may discuss are: the role of affective conditioning in advertising, the use pervasiveness of advertising, various advertising techniques, the use of Photoshopping, targeted marketing, and 360° integrated marketing.

Student Poll (p. 331): Answers will vary. Students are asked to evaluate how effective advertising is on influencing their desires, wants, and choices. We are once again having students look at their relationship to advertising. It would be interesting to ask them if they feel their answers about how advertising affects them have changed over the course of the chapter.

4. **Whatever Works** (p. 332): Answers will vary. This scenario asks students to explain their position on the practice by some advertisers of pairing sex and violence in advertising. This question requires students to evaluate the use of sex and violence in advertising, weigh the pros and cons, and then articulate their own position regarding this topic.

Student Poll (p. 332): Answers will vary. Students are asked to evaluate how they feel about the position that advertising should have no limits placed on it in terms of what is shocking and sensational, especially since it does what advertising is supposed to do: get ads noticed and remembered. In a discussion about this poll, the class needs to also discuss how such ads might backfire by transferring negative feelings to the brand, the possible societal consequences of such advertising, how brands can affect our behavior, and the use of Photoshopping and its impact on us.

5. **Billboard Ad** (p. 333): Designs will vary. Students have the opportunity to create their own ad about anything they would like to share with other people. This is their own PSA. This activity will be used in 7.11.

7.11   (pages 334-336)

1. **My Best and Worst Ads** (p. 334): Answers will vary. Students will work in small groups to share their favorite and least favorite ads. They are to discuss the "why" behind their selections and see if their rationale has changed due to what they have learned. This activity allows students to share their preferences, engage in communicating the reasons for their choices, discuss what they have learned and how what they have learned may reshape the reasons for their choices, and discuss how advertising techniques may have shaped their preferences (or failed to when it comes to their least favorite ad).

2. **To Photoshop or Not?** (p. 334): Answers will vary. Students work in small groups to discuss a scenario that focuses on the use of real-sized models and the Photoshopping of models in advertising. Students must decide as advertising associates what to recommend to their boss about the use of real-sized models and the Photoshopping of models. This will get them to discuss the pros and cons with one another and then work together to come up with a recommendation they all agree on. This activity requires them to identify the pros and cons, evaluate them, and work together to create a consensus.

3. **Does Advertising Determine Your Tastes?** (p. 334): Answers will vary. This activity piggy-backs on activity #3 in 7.10 and brings it into a debate. Either assign #3 in 7.10 as homework or class work prior to the debate. The teacher may want to allow the two sides to meet together to develop their strategy and topics. The teacher may also want to provide each side with some prompts if they need it to aid in their discussion.

4. **Creating an Ad** (p. 335): Answers will vary. Students will work in small groups with one small group selected to be the client and the others to be the ad agencies. Each group will pitch two print ads, one for each product. In their groups they will work to create the ads and their presentation. Each group presents their ads and then the client selects the winning ad for each product. This activity has the students work together in applying what they have learned about advertising to create effective print ads. The client group works together to create their criteria for evaluating the ads, which gets them to consider what makes an effective and successful ad. This is a fun, interactive way to immerse students in the content of the chapter. It will create plenty of content for a large group discussion.

5. **Whatever Works** (p. 335): This activity focuses on the statement that they rated in the Student Poll in activity #4 in 7.10. Have a large group discussion about the use of shocking and sensational content in advertising. Consider making a list of the pros and cons on something the whole class can see. Discuss the impact on society and culture. See how that relates to the class's list of pros and cons and to them personally. It will be important to make sure students remain respectful in how they disagree.

6. **Billboard Ads** (p. 336): Begin in small groups with the students sharing their billboard and the impact they hope the billboard would have on viewers. Then have the class look at each other's billboards. You can do this by having them leave their billboard on their desk and have an Art Walk, or you could have them display their billboard on the walls in the room, or you could use some other means.

Following the Art Walk, discuss the billboards. Ask the students which ones stood out for them and why. Consider having students volunteer to talk about their billboards and what it meant to them to create one. Discuss what impact PSAs in general have on society. Perhaps consider a class project of selecting one or more of the billboards and finding a way to display them on campus.

7. **Cool Hunters** (p. 336): The focus here is on 7.8 and marketing to teens. One of the ways this occurs is through appealing to the desire of teens to be cool. The topic should lend itself to an interesting discussion about what it means to be cool, who gets to decide what is cool, what if you aren't cool, how they convey to other people what is cool, and how cool is marketed to teens. Discuss if they like that their online identity is also advertisement for corporations. The polls in 7.8 could be brought into this discussion. It might also be helpful to focus on whether or not trying to gain "Likes" leads to conformity and forces them to reshape who they are so they will be "Liked." A great question is: Can you really be yourself if you are worried about "Likes"?

8. **Generation Like** (p. 336): Consider showing the whole 53-minute documentary of Generation Like to your class and using some of the discussion questions from activity #7 "Cool Hunters" or develop some of your own.

Chapter 8
Eyewitness Testimony, Direct & Circumstantial Evidence

8.1   (pages 337-338)

Student Poll (p. 337): Answers will vary. Students are to rate the importance of understanding direct and circumstantial evidence, particularly eyewitness testimony, for critical thinkers and explain their rating. This has them utilize the cognitive skills of comprehension, analysis, and evaluation. It also gets them to personally own how important (or not) they feel that circumstantial evidence and direct evidence are for critical thinkers.

Prediction (p. 338): Predictions will vary. Students will need to use their cognitive skills to relate the picture with the topic. This will also facilitate buy-in.

8.2   (page 339)

Student Poll: The direct evidence items are: eyewitness testimony, confessions, surveillance tapes, receipts, and physical evidence. Examples of physical evidence are a bullet casing, bloody shirt, knife, or gun.

8.3   (page 340)

The "Which Is Which" Quiz

1. direct evidence; The witness claims to have seen the rain herself on the night of the murder.

2. indirect evidence; The witness made an inference that it was raining the night of the murder based on seeing a man come into the diner wearing a raincoat and seeing that it had water drops on it. Her conclusion is not based on any direct experience of it raining, such as looking out a window at the rain or going outside and seeing it rain.

8.4   (pages 341-346)

Student Poll (p. 341): Answers will vary. Students are asked to evaluate the statements and select the one that they think is the most accurate in regards to direct and circumstantial evidence. This poll functions as a preassessment for the students. Many of them may be surprised to learn that either one can be used to establish guilt and that both carry equal weight in the United States legal system.

Evidence and Inference Practice (pp. 342-344)

1. Types of evidence: Direct evidence: dead body with a gunshot wound to the head; eyewitness testimony by Leigh that two men, one with a gun, abducted Wise, forcing him into the trunk of a blue 1985 Oldsmobile. Circumstantial evidence: the bullet from a .40 Smith & Wesson recovered from the head of the victim, the red handkerchief used as a gag, the angry behavior of the two men when they confronted Wise, Leigh's eyewitness testimony that the shorter man fired his gun in the air twice, the two spent shell casing recovered at the scene of the abduction and that were from a Smith and Wesson type firearm. Note: Leigh's eyewitness testimony that the shorter man fired his gun in the air is circumstantial because it does not directly prove that he committed the murder or that the two spent shell casings recovered in the parking lot at the scene of the abduction were from his gun.

Inferences: (1) Given the behavior of the two men when they confronted Wise, the presence of the gun, and the abduction, we can infer that they meant to hurt Wise. (2) Given that the two men were wearing black gloves on a very hot day—which was unusual enough that both witnesses remarked that it was odd—and that a gun was used in the abduction, we could infer that they did not want to leave fingerprints behind when they did something illegal. (3) Given that the two men were very angry with Wise; that the shorter of the men had a gun and fired it twice in a public place; that the two men abducted Wise, forcing him into the trunk of the car; that they wearing black gloves on a very hot day—perhaps to not leave fingerprints; that a red handkerchief like the one worn by the taller man was found at the crime scene; that the spent shell casings were from a .40 Smith and Wesson gun, and that Wise died from a gunshot to the head by a .40 Smith and Wesson gun, we can infer that both men were involved in the murder.

2. Types of evidence: Direct evidence: There is none. Circumstantial evidence: The make of the car that matches the make used in the kidnapping of Wise; Maze's clothing matches the clothing of the shorter man involved in the kidnapping of Wise, who had the gun, fired the gun twice, and who drove the blue 1985 Oldsmobile in the abduction of Wise; the black gloves with the gunshot residue on them; the black shirt with blood splatter and gunshot residue on it; the blood on the shirt that matches the blood type of the victim, which was AB+ (only 3% of people in the U.S. have this type of blood); and the strand of hair that matches that of the victim in the trunk of the blue 1985 Oldsmobile that Maze was driving.

Inferences: (1) The blue 1985 Oldsmobile that Maze was driving is the same car used in the kidnapping of Wise. (2) The strand of hair in the trunk corroborates that this is the same car used in the kidnapping. (3) Maze is the shorter man seen by Leigh (the clothes and gloves support this) who had the gun, fired it twice, was involved in the abduction of Wise, and drove the car that use used in the kidnapping. (4) Maze was involved in the murder of Wise, perhaps even the one who directly killed him. The evidence for this: the gunshot residue shows that Maze fired a gun (though that may only be from firing it in the late afternoon), the bullet casings found where the abduction occurred and the bullet removed from the head of the victim are of the same caliber—.40 Smith and Wesson, Maze had a .40 Smith and Wesson that he fired at the site of the kidnapping, the shirt that he was wearing had blood splatter of the same blood type as the victim (which was AB+ and the type that only 3% of the U.S. population and thus increasing the probability that it was from the victim), and the strand of hair that matched that of the victim was found in the trunk of his car (showing that the victim was in his car and the car could have been the how the victim was transported to the wooded area of the murder). It seems Maze had means to commit the murder as well as the opportunity.

3. Types of Evidence: Direct – The gun registration proves that he owned the .40 Smith and Wesson found in his garage. Circumstantial – The .40 Smith and Wesson gun found hidden in Maze's garage in a box of Christmas decorations, the .40 Smith and Wesson bullet removed from the head of the victim, and the ballistic match of the bullet that killed Wise to the gun found in Maze's garage and the ballistic match of the bullets at the scene of the kidnapping to the gun found in Maze's garage.

Inferences: (1) Maze hid the gun in the box of Christmas decorations in his garage because he did not want it found. (2) The bullet that killed Wise came from Maze's gun. (3) Maze's gun is the murder weapon. (4) Maze is the one who actually murdered Wise. He had the means and the opportunity to do it, and while we don't know of a specific motive, we do know he was very angry and involved in assaulting (pushing) Wise before the abduction. There is direct evidence that he owned the murder weapon (circumstantial evidence establishes it as the murder weapon). There is strong circumstantial evidence that he is the one to shoot Wise: He demonstrated suspicious behavior by hiding the .40 Smith and Wesson gun he owned, the bullet that killed Wise and removed from his head was a ballistic match to Maze's gun, Maze is the one who was seen handling and firing the gun during the abduction and the two spent bullet casings were matched to his gun, the gunshot residue on his shirt and gloves shows that he fired his gun, the blood splatter that matches the victim's blood type was found on this shirt and shows that he was in close proximity to the victim when he was killed.

4. Maze: Kidnapping – Guilty, Murder – Guilty; Robinson: Kidnapping: Guilty; Murder – Guilty

Direct evidence (eyewitness testimony by Leigh and a confession by Robinson that they both were involved in the kidnapping) establishes that the two men kidnapped Wise, and the strand of hair in the trunk is circumstantial evidence that further supports that they kidnapped Wise. Direct evidence (eyewitness testimony by Robinson) stablishes that Maze killed Wise. There is strong circumstantial evidence that corroborates that Maze murdered Wise, which was reviewed in question #3. Robinson admits in a confession that he was part of the kidnapping, which is a felony, and that he saw Maze shoot Robinson. Since the crime occurred in a state where if a murder occurs during a felony crime, then all those involved in the crime are equally responsible for the murder, it does not matter whether or not Robinson wanted Wise killed or helped to plan the murder, he is also responsible for committing the murder. So both men are guilty of kidnapping and murder. If Robinson can show that he did not want Wise killed and had no idea that Wise would be murdered, then his sentence might be different than Maze's sentence; for example if they are in a state that has the death penalty, Maze might be sentenced to death but Robinson to life without parole.

Prediction Revision (p. 344): Students have the opportunity to think further about what the image might have to do with the topic of eyewitness testimony and circumstantial and direct evidence.

Evidence Quiz (pp. 345-346)

1. Guilty; There is overwhelming circumstantial evidence that he committed the crime. The circumstantial evidence is the witness's testimony that she saw Mr. Thomas covered in blood and carrying a gun immediately after hearing gunfire outside the store where Mr. Simms was found dead (To be direct evidence, the witness would need to see Mr. Thomas shoot Mr. Simms), the blood on Mr. Simms was the victim's blood, the bullet recovered from the body of Mr. Simms was matched to the gun Mr. Thomas was carrying, and there was gunshot residue on Mr. Thomas's hand.

2. Guilty; There is both direct and circumstantial evidence that he committed the crime. The direct evidence is the eyewitness testimony of both Mrs. Ames and John Willard. Mrs. Ames provides direct testimony that the Jake Winston is the man who approached her for money and then knocked her down and stole her purse. John Willard also provides direct evidence that he saw Jake Winston knock Mrs. Ames down and run off with the purse. Both independently identified Jake Winston in the lineup as the man who committed the crime. The circumstantial evidence supports the direct evidence that Jake Winston committed the crime. This circumstantial evidence is that he was found running from the scene of the crime, he was found in the proximity of the scene of the crime (one block away), and he matched the description of the suspect: a white man in his early twenties wearing a grey hoodie and jeans.

Check-in (p. 346): Encourage the students to seek coaching if they select the unhappy kitty. These check-ins are important for student self-assessments and creating personal accountability for their learning.

8.5   (pages 347-352)

The Power of Eyewitness Testimony Thought Experiment (p. 347): Answers may vary, but the students need to discuss why they think eyewitness testimony is powerful and evaluate if it deserves this kind of power. Eyewitness testimony is powerful because we believe that we see everything around us, that we remember it accurately, and that what we remember represents reality, so if a witness sees X do Y, then X must have done Y. Why do we believe this? Because many of us believe that what we see is recorded accurately and completely by our memory; in other words, our memory functions like a video recorder. We do not realize that we do not see everything; in fact, we often miss changes in our visual world from one view to the next and as a consequence, we fill in gaps in our memory in order to create meaning. Unfortunately, this filler is based on our assumptions, which may not always be accurate. Our chapter will show that there are a number of good reasons why eyewitness testimony should not have this kind of power—all of which demonstrate how unreliable it can be. Circumstantial evidence is actually much more reliable.

Student Poll (p. 348): Students are identifying their beliefs about their memory, which they can reflect upon as they study how their memory actually works.

The Selective Attention Thought Experiment (p. 350): 15; 15; Various answers, but the takeaway is that we do not always see everything. For students who did not see the gorilla, this takeaway should be fairly obvious, but for those that did see the gorilla, the question asked "But did you see the gorilla?!" should be a clue that perhaps some people do not see the gorilla, and as a result, their takeaway may be that sometimes we do not see everything. The goal is for the students to do some critical thinking around their experience of this video.

Student Poll (p. 350): Answers will vary. This poll primes the students for the two Thought Experiments that follow and for the examination of the reliability of eyewitness testimony.

The Change Blindness Thought Experiment 1 (p. 351): Answers vary as to how the students did in the experiment.

1. a; 2. b

The reason people fail to notice the switch in men has to do with attention—or what we are focused on. This occurs because when we look at a person we encode what is relevant to what we are doing right at that moment, which in the experiment is giving directions. We do not pay attention to details that are irrelevant, which in this case might be the color of the man's shirt or even how tall he is. Our goal is basically to make meaning of the scene and roughly the main categories of that person (sex, race, old or young etc.). If these irrelevant details change but do not affect the meaning of the scene, then we may not notice anything different. We think we are aware of all of the details of everything around us and that if something important happens, then we will notice it. As Dr. Simons points out, the reality is that we are unaware of a lot more of our world than we think we are, so we often fail to notice unexpected things.

True

The Change Blindness Thought Experiment 2 (p. 352): The unusual thing that happened after the people signed the consent form was that the person waiting on them changed; 75%. In this last question, the experiment is a means for getting the students to think about change blindness. Most will probably be surprised by the number of people who did not notice the change. This question would make an excellent start for a class discussion. It may, also, be a question to revisit as the students study eyewitness testimony, especially asking what change blindness might mean for eyewitness testimony.

8.6   (pages 353-358)

The Eyewitness Testimony Thought Experiment (p. 353): Answers may vary, but what the students have learned already should raise some flags about the reliability of eyewitness testimony since memory isn't like a video recorder and we often miss things. This activity primes students for the discussion on the reliability of eyewitness testimony that will follow.

The "Getting It Right" Thought Experiment (pp. 356-357)

1. Jennifer Thompson felt she would be able to identify her assailant because she paid attention to his face, hair, voice, clothes, and weight. She felt she had memorized everything about him.

2. At the photographic lineup, Jennifer felt her job was to find the perpetrator in the photo lineup.

3. She spent 4-5 minutes going back and forth between two photos. While she wanted to be certain, the fact that she was struggling between two photos shows that she was not certain enough to recognize her assailant immediately.

4. Yes, something did happen after the lineup to boost her confidence about her identification—it was the feedback she received immediately after the identification. She said she felt relief that she got the identification right.

5. These studies show that when people get positive feedback around identification, then their "confidence skyrocketed."

6. She would feel even more confident about her identification. Studies have shown that repeating only one individual in multiple procedures increases witness confidence even when the witness is wrong about the identification.

7. After the lineup, Jennifer asked, "How did I do? Did I do ok?" The officer told her, "You did great—that was the guy who you picked out in the photographic lineup." At the trial she was 100% certain. All the reinforcement that she had received in terms of correctly identifying the perpetrator of the crime made her feel she was 100% certain.

8. Ronald Cotton Jr. spent 11 years in prison for a crime he did not commit. DNA was used to exonerate him.

9. Student answers will vary. They need to explain their reasons for allowing or not allowing eyewitness testimony as evidence in a trial.

Student Poll (p. 358): Students are asked to evaluate how reliable they feel the solutions make eyewitness identification. This will require them to use their critical thinking skills of comprehension and analysis.

8.7   (pages 359-361)

Important Takeaways (p. 361): The students need to think about how direct and circumstantial evidence impacts their lives and to identify three takeaways that they want to remember.

8.8   (pages 362-365)

1. **Recall Challenge** (p. 362): Students are asked to write down as many of the 20 items as they can remember. This activity shows them some of the limits of their memory. The items are: butterfly, toothbrush, dog, chair, flower, car, kite, ice cream cone, hat, guitar, smartphone, skateboard, apple, cupcake, tree, bird, clock, monkey, key, ring.

2. **Perception Test I** (p. 363): The lines are the same size.

3. **Perception Test II** (p. 363): All the color palettes are the same.

4. **The Crime Scene!** (p. 365): The pictures below show the 10 differences between the two crime scene photos.

Crime Scene Photo 1   Crime Scene Photo 2

The clock, the wall calendar, the gun, the shirt hanging off the chair and the slippers on the floor seen in Crime Scene Photo 1 have been removed in Crime Scene Photo 2. The phone has been moved from the desk at front in photo 1 to the computer tower in front of the bed (where the gun was previously seen) in photo 2. The glass of water on the back computer desk in photo 1 has been replaced with a can of Coke in photo 2. A roll of duct tape, a pocket knife and a pair of gloves not seen in photo 1 have been introduced in photo 2. Most students are likely to find at least seven differences. Not many are likely to find the slippers.

8.9   (pages 366-371)

1. **The Case of the Murder of Robert Head**

   The Investigation (p. 366): The jury must vote on whether or not Maurice Patterson is guilty of murder, and then they need to explain why they voted the way they did. Students will most likely vote "Yes" because of the number of eyewitnesses who claim to have witnessed the fight that occurred between Robert Head and the assailant. But is the eyewitness testimony enough to convict him? How certain are these witnesses? Under what conditions did they observe the fight? There is also the bloody knife found near the scene—how does it impact the case? Are there fingerprints on it? Is so, do they belong to Maurice Patterson? Was blood found on his clothes? Does Maurice have an alibi? There are many questions such as these that need to be answered. The best answer for the jury is "Undecided" at this time; however, this should not be conveyed to the students as this would circumvent the value of the activity. The process will work best if students work all the way through the activity BEFORE there is any class discussion.

The Eyewitness Testimony (p. 367): The jury must vote on whether or not Maurice Patterson is guilty of murder based on the new evidence, and if they changed their vote, they must explain why. What is telling here is the lack of confidence the three witness have that they have identified the correct person; in fact, they have to be threatened with Contempt of Court in order to make them testify. We also now have some information about the conditions under which they glimpsed the fight: it was in the dark, and we learn that they only had a "fleeting glimpse" of the fight. This makes their eyewitness testimony highly suspect and undermines how accurate it is. Is it really sufficient enough to convict someone of murder? The best answer at this point is "Undecided."

The DNA Evidence (pp. 367-368): The jury must vote on whether or not Maurice Patterson is guilty of murder based on the new DNA evidence, and if they changed their vote, they must explain why. Based on the DNA evidence Maurice Patterson did not commit the murder—someone else did. Unfortunately, because the DNA results were never directly sent to the Cook County State's Attorney's Office, they excluded the knife as the murder weapon and continued the case against Maurice Patterson. Why didn't they pursue this information themselves? We need to also ask if Patterson's lawyer even knew about the knife. He or she should have. If not, why not? If so, then why didn't the lawyer pursue the results?

The Trial – the Alibi (p. 368): The jury must vote on if it would have made a difference to them as to whether or not Maurice Patterson's family testified in regards to his alibi, and the jury must explain why. This information should make a difference to the jury. While they must weigh whether or not the wife and stepdaughters are credible witnesses, it should at least raise some questions about the eyewitness testimony or, at the very least, make it warrant a second look. Why didn't Patterson's trial counsel call them to testify? Was his lawyer incompetent or overburdened? Bad lawyering is one of the causes for the conviction of innocent people—often people who do not have the money to hire a lawyer but must depend on a public defender or court-appointed attorney. As the Innocence Project explains, "Shrinking funding and access to resources for public defenders and court-appointed attorneys is only making the problem [conviction of innocent people] worse."

The Trial – Other Defense Testimony (p. 369): The jury must vote on if it would have made a difference to them whether or not Maurice Patterson testified, and they need to explain why. Often for defense attorneys the issue is how well the defendant will do on the stand. Good attorneys weigh this when making their determination as well as if it is necessary—often they choose not to when they feel that not enough information has been presented at the trial to convict their client. Also, we have the issue of whether Patterson had a lawyer who was not performing his or her job adequately. Were there other people that could have been called, such as character witnesses, for Patterson who could vouch for him? Did Patterson want to speak? Often juries do want to hear from the defendant. Given that the jury has only the eyewitness testimony—and may not know how suspect it is, it may have made a difference if Patterson had testified.

The Trial – The Prosecution (p. 369): The jury now has all the evidence. They are to vote on whether or not they think Maurice Patterson committed the murder. Then the jury needs to explain the reasoning behind their decision. Note: The prosecution chose to ignore the knife because they claimed no DNA from the victim was found on it. We were told in the case that the Cook County State's Attorney's Office was never directly notified by the Police Forensic Science Center that the sample from the bloody knife included the victim's blood, which—along with the its proximity to the murder— would lead to a reasonable conclusion that the knife is the murder weapon. The issue arises that while the State's Attorney's Office was not directly contacted about the victim's DNA on the knife, they did have access to this information indirectly which should have prompted them to contact the Police Forensic Science Center. Why didn't they pursue the results on their own? Why didn't they call the Police Forensic Science Center when they did not hear anything? They knew how bad their eyewitness testimony was. This should have prompted them to seek the results and do all they could to see that an innocent man was not convicted of murder. Our case information does not provide the answer to these questions, but it is a reasonable to raise them. Ultimately, if the prosecution knew about the forensic results (however they got them), then that leads to further questions as to why they proceeded with the trial.

CNN Jury Interview (p. 369): The jury members need to identify and clearly articulate their reasoning in regards to the verdict. Consider a large group discussion about whether anyone felt pressured to go along with the other students on their jury, and if they did feel pressured, did they actually vote for a verdict they did not believe in or where uncertain of. Ask them, "What could you have done to feel more confident in your position and vote?" Discuss how people might feel pressured on a real jury.

The Actual Verdict (p. 370): Each student is to answer the question "What did you think of the actual verdict?" Then, as a group, they are to discuss what they thought of the actual verdict. This allows them to possibly hear differing points of view. They also need to spend time brainstorming what could be done within the criminal justice system to prevent wrongful convictions.

The Jury and Critical Thinking (p. 370): The jury is to discuss what importance, if any, critical thinking plays for jury members. They are to summarize their conclusion and present them to the class. See #4 of the large group discussion.

Large group discussion (p. 370)

1. The DNA evidence on the bloody knife, which is the murder weapon, was the evidence critical to the case. There was no DNA evidence from Maurice Patterson on the knife, so the results excluded Maurice Patterson. The DNA evidence did indicate a mixture of the victim's profile and an unknown profile, which they were able to identify as belonging to a drug addict with a violent history. This evidence was critical to the case because it excludes Maurice Patterson as the perpetrator and clearly points to another suspect. Based on the DNA evidence Maurice Patterson should not have been put on trial for the murder of Robert Head. This case clearly raises other issues about eyewitness testimony—which in this case was unreliable—proper representation, the impact of wealth in the court system (if Maurice would have had money, then he would not have had to depend on a public defender but rather someone dedicated to representing him), race, and about proper procedures (the failure of the Police Forensic Science Center to not directly notify the Cook County State's Attorney's Office of the DNA results—which raises the issue of whether this was an unusual circumstance or whether this happens regularly or at least occurs enough to make other convictions that depend on this organization for results suspect. At the very least, this situation should be

investigated as to why the Police Forensic Science Center failed to provide notification of the results to the Cook County State's Attorney's Office).

2. The students probably found that their votes changed as they received more information. The new information helps them evaluate the information relative to the question of guilt or innocence. They, also, probably found the eyewitness testimony unreliable given the dark night and the very short time the witnesses had to see the perpetrator and the victim. The DNA evidence would more than likely cause the jury to re-evaluate any guilty verdict.

3. The safeguards that could have been put in place to help prevent a wrongful conviction are a sequential double-blind procedure for identification, a blank lineup, making use of fillers that resemble the eyewitness description, confidence statements, changing the identification instructions of the lineup to say that the perpetrator may not be present, and a system which cross-checks notification of forensic results from the Police Forensic Science Center to the Cook County State's Attorney's Office and to all parties that are authorized to receive them. One additional safeguard would be to see that defendants are properly represented and that their public defender or court-appointed lawyer has all the necessary resources that he or she needs in order to mount a defense.

4. Critical thinking is essential to any member of the jury because it makes use of the cognitive skills that are necessary in the work of the jury: comprehension, analysis, evaluation, and communication. Juries need to use these skills in evaluating evidence so that they can arrive at a just verdict, and so they can communicate in a discussion, whether it is to raise questions, analyze evidence, or explain their positions. In addition, because critical thinking makes use of reason, it helps prevent jury members from being swept away by an emotional response to the case and neglect the evidence.

Part II
Reproducible Activities

Reproducible Activities

Chapter 1 .... R1-R15
  1.1 Why Care About Critical Thinking? R1
  1.2 What Is Critical Thinking? R3
  1.3 What Makes ME a Critical Thinker? R5
  1.4 Obstacles to Critical Thinking R6
  1.5 Important Takeaways R12
  1.6 Individual Activities R13

Chapter 2 .... R16-R33
  2.1 Why Practice? R16
  2.2 Smarty Pants Puzzles™ R17
  2.3 Classroom Quickies™ R20
  2.4 Seven Chairs R21
  2.5 Dr. Funster's Visual Mind Benders® R22
  2.6 Mind Benders® R27
  2.7 Important Takeaways R33

Chapter 3 .... R34-R53
  3.1 My CT Tool Box R34
  3.2 Facts vs. Opinions R35
  3.3 Possible, Probable, and Proven R38
  3.4 Evidence R40
  3.5 Creativity, Creative Thinking,
       & Creative Problem Solving R43
  3.6 Important Takeaways R47
  3.7 Individual Activities R48
  3.8 Group Activities & Discussion R50

Chapter 4 .... R54-R78
  4.1 Emotional Words and Arguments R54
  4.2 The Problem With Ambiguity R61
  4.3 Vagueness R65
  4.4 Doublespeak: Euphemism & Jargon R68
  4.5 Doublespeak: Gobbledygook
       & Inflated Language R72
  4.6 Important Takeaways R74
  4.7 Individual Activities R75

Chapter 5 .... R79-R121
  5.1 What's Up With Arguments R79
  5.2 What Is an Argument? R80
  5.3 Recognizing Arguments R84

  5.4 Deductive Arguments R87
  5.5 Inductive Arguments R90
  5.6 Evaluating Deductive Arguments R96
  5.7 Evaluating Inductive Arguments R104
  5.8 Important Takeaways R113
  5.9 Individual Activities R114
  5.10 Group Activities & Discussion R117

Chapter 6 .... R122-R156
  6.1 What Are Fallacies? R122
  6.2 Fallacies of Relevance R123
  6.3 Fallacies of Presumption R128
  6.4 Fallacies of Weak Induction R133
  6.5 Fallacies of Ambiguity R138
  6.6 Detecting and Avoiding Fallacies R144
  6.7 Important Takeaways R150
  6.8 Individual Activities R151
  6.9 Group Activities & Discussion R155

Chapter 7 .... R157-R202
  7.1 Introduction R157
  7.2 The Pros and Cons of Advertising R158
  7.3 What Do Ads Do? R173
  7.4 How Ads Persuade Us: The Backstory R174
  7.5 Advertising Techniques R175
  7.6 Regulated Advertising R193
  7.8 "Cool Hunting" R194
  7.9 Important Takeaways R195
  7.10 Individual Activities R196
  7.11 Group Activities & Discussion R202

Chapter 8 .... R203-R230
  8.1 Introduction R203
  8.2 What Is Direct Evidence? R204
  8.3 What Is Circumstantial Evidence? R205
  8.4 A Closer Look R206
  8.5 Eyewitness Testimony and Memory R212
  8.6 The Reliability of Eyewitness Testimony R216
  8.7 Important Takeaways R220
  8.8 Individual Activities R221
  8.9 Group Activities & Discussion R225

1.1 Why Care About Critical Thinking?

A World Without Critical Thinking Thought Experiment (p. 1): Imagine waking up tomorrow and everyone around the world is no longer engaged in critical thinking. Not even you! What would that mean? How would you behave? How would those around you behave, such as your family, friends, or people at your school? While we haven't defined critical thinking yet, you probably have some idea that it involves the use of reason, good judgment, and logic. So imagine that everyone no longer uses these skills as they go about making decisions. Do you think you'd be able to make good decisions? Would not having critical thinking skills improve your chance for success in life? Would it make you less vulnerable to outside influences and manipulation in your life? Would you be less susceptible to advertising and propaganda? What about the impact on society? Would it make us better voters? Better jurors? Better parents? Better business owners? Better doctors or nurses? Better world leaders?

Here's what I think: _____

_____

_____

_____

Prediction Time (p. 3)

From time to time you will be asked to make a prediction about something related to what we are learning. You can always change your prediction. Here's our very first one!

The Anatomy of the Teen Brain

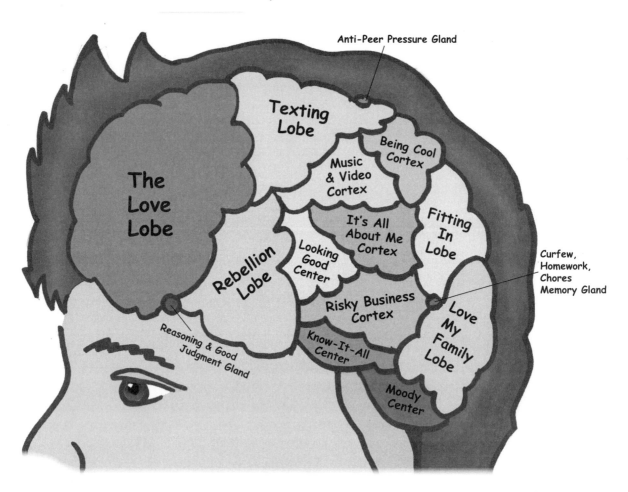

My Prediction

I think you'll be telling me about _____

_____

1.2 What Is Critical Thinking?

Critical Thinking Skills Quiz (p. 4): Place a check mark next to critical thinking skills we have learned about in section 1.1.

_____ Creativity

_____ Writing

_____ Analysis

_____ Thinking

_____ Construction

_____ Reading

_____ Comprehension

_____ Laughing

_____ Evaluation

_____ Communication

When you are done, turn back to section 1.1 and check your answers. How well did you do?

Activity Thought Experiment (p. 4): Think of an activity you like to do. Perhaps it is an activity such as shooting free throws, skateboarding, surfing, playing soccer, dancing, writing stories, playing a particular video game, or painting.

My activity is: _____

Were you great the first time you did this activity? _____

Did you need to practice to get better at it? _____

What would happen if you quit practicing? _____

_____

Would you do this activity as well as before if you quit practicing? _____

Do you need to revise your prediction? If so, do it here. (p. 5)

_____

_____

"What is Critical Thinking?" Thought Experiment (p. 5): In the space below, design a webpage that explains what critical thinking is based on what you have learned so far and why it is important.

1.3 What Makes ME a Critical Thinker?

⭐ **Student Poll** (p. 6): Read this true story from the February 2007 *Reader's Digest*:

> Because patient files are confidential, the government requires that
>
> our hospital keep them safe from prying eyes. Hence, this sign at
>
> the nurses' station just off a heavily traveled corridor: "All patient
>
> information is kept locked up. It is in the locker in the top corner.
>
> The combination is 32, 16, 24."

On a scale from 1 ("Extremely bad!") to 10 ("Fantastic!") rate the critical thinking going on in this story. _____

1.4 Obstacles to Critical Thinking

⭐ **Student Poll** (p. 8): On a scale from 1 ("Not surprised!") to 10 ("Are you kidding me?"), rate how surprised you are about your brain development.

My surprise number is: _____

💡 **"I Could Have Done Better" Thought Experiment** (p. 8): Think about a time when you needed to use critical thinking, but you didn't do so well using it. Why do you think that happened? What do you think might have been an obstacle to your critical thinking?

_____

_____

_____

_____

Egocentrism

Egocentrism Obstacle (p. 9)

Why would egocentrism be an obstacle? Write your answer to this question now:

_____

_____

_____

Egocentrism Thought Experiment (p. 9): If one of your friends came to you and said that he was having problems with the obstacle of egocentrism, what would you suggest he do to overcome this obstacle or to not let it get the best of him?

_____

_____

_____

_____

Peer pressure

⭐ **Student Poll** (p. 10): Check the ways that your peers have had a positive influence on you.

_____ Shared music with me

_____ Gave me advice

_____ Invited me to join a club

_____ Helped me with my homework

_____ Listened to a problem I had

_____ Taught me a new skill

_____ Encouraged me to try out for a sport or an activity

_____ Stood up for me

💡 **Peer Pressure Thought Experiment** (p. 11): You've been asked by the art teacher to make a poster for your school of some tips to help kids deal with peer pressure. Come up with four tips to include on this poster and think of a catchy phrase or slogan (or graphic) you might include to catch everyone's attention about peer pressure.

Tip 1 _____

Tip 2 _____

Tip 3 _____

Tip 4 _____

Slogan or graphic ideas: _____

_____

_____

Unreasonable Assumptions

Assumption Thought Experiment (p. 12):   Today I made this assumption:

_____

_____

_____

What would have happened if you hadn't made this assumption? If you had been forced to wait until you had proof before you could act?

_____

_____

_____

Student Poll (p. 13): On a scale from 1 ("All the time!") to 10 ("Never, I'm perfect!"), rate how often you make unreasonable assumptions. _____

Emotion

 Emotion and Critical Thinking Practice I (p. 14)

What do you think is going on? _____

_____

Do you think the emotion they are feeling will probably help or hurt their critical thinking?

_____ Help   _____ Hurt

Explain why. _____

_____

_____

Emotion and Critical Thinking Practice II (p. 15)

What is going on in this picture? _____

_____

Do you think the emotion she is feeling will probably help or hurt her critical thinking?

_____ Help   _____ Hurt

Explain why. _____

_____

_____

⭐ **Student Poll** (p. 16): On a scale of 1 ("Never! Never! Never!") to 10 ("All the time—it's so annoying!"), rate your experience with these critical thinking obstacles.

_____ My brain		_____ Self-interest
_____ Peer pressure		_____ Self-serving bias
_____ Stereotypes		_____ Emotion

Important Takeaways

Three important takeaways that I want to remember from this chapter are:

1. _____

_____

_____

2. _____

_____

_____

3. _____

_____

_____

1.6 Individual Activities

1. **The Best Critical Thinkers I Know** (p. 20)

    Who are the best critical thinkers that you know? (List at least three people.)

    _____

    _____

    _____

    Explain why you think they are good critical thinkers—be specific.

    _____

    _____

    _____

    _____

    _____

    _____

    _____

    _____

    _____

    _____

    Write a description of a good critical thinker based on why you think these people are good critical thinkers.

    _____

    _____

    _____

    _____

2. **Insanity and Albert Einstein** (p. 21)

Albert Einstein (a theoretical physicist who is considered one the most influential physicists of the 20th century) said: "Insanity is doing the same thing over and over again while expecting a different outcome."

What do you think this quote has to do with critical thinking?

_____

_____

_____

_____

_____

_____

3. **Pumping Up** (p. 21)

Explain what this picture has to do with what makes you a critical thinker?

_____

_____

_____

4. **My Top Two Obstacles To Critical Thinking** (p. 22)
Rank the list of critical thinking obstacles according to your own experience from 1 (the obstacle that happens a lot) to 5 (the obstacle that happens less often).

_____ The teen brain

_____ Egocentrism

_____ Peer pressure

_____ Unreasonable assumptions (including stereotypes)

_____ Emotion

My number 1 obstacle to critical thinking is: _____

because _____

_____

Here's what I want to do to work on making this less of an obstacle:

_____

_____

_____

My number 2 obstacle to critical thinking is: _____

because _____

_____

Here's what I want to do to work on making this less of an obstacle:

_____

_____

_____

2.1 Why Practice

My Brain Tattoo (p. 26): A brain tattoo is a tool for helping you etch, or tattoo, something into your mind so you'll remember it. Draw an image or poster, or write out this message in a way that will ensure you remember it: **Our ability as critical thinkers grows in proportion to our use of our critical thinking skills—the more we use them, the better we are at critical thinking.** You can design it any way you want and use the words or symbols that will help you remember this important message.

2.2 Smarty Pants Puzzles™*

General Information

These puzzles require you to determine, based on the evidence, what you know with certainty to be true or false and/or what might be probably true or probably false depending upon the puzzle. You also have to determine when you do not have enough evidence to draw a conclusion.

Footprints (p. 27)

The footprints that Ted saw.

¹Ted went to the beach with his older brother George on Saturday. ²George drove and found a parking space close to the water. ³Both he and his brother love going swimming at the beach. ⁴It was a warm, sunny day and Ted fell asleep after swimming in the water. ⁵When he woke up he couldn't find his brother, although George's car keys and towel were still there. ⁶He got up and looked around, but all he could see were footprints. ⁷There didn't appear to be anyone on the beach, but the car was still in the parking lot. ⁸Ted also knew that George would never leave him alone at the beach with no way home. ⁹Ted concluded that George had gone swimming.

Assume all the statements and facts in the puzzle are true. Write whether each sentence is **T**rue, **F**alse, or **U**nknown. Then write the sentence number(s) and/or check the box that provides the best evidence for each true or false answer.

_____ 1. The footprints that Ted saw lead away from the water.

    ____   ☐   ☐

    Sentence   Picture   Caption

_____ 2. Ted couldn't find his brother, and he didn't see anyone on the beach.

    ____ ____ ____   ☐   ☐

    Sentences   Picture   Caption

_____ 3. George didn't go swimming with Ted.

    ____   ☐   ☐

    Sentence   Picture   Caption

_____ 4. Ted's conclusion that George has gone swimming is most likely true.

    ____ ____ ____ ____ ____   ☐   ☐

    Sentences   Picture   Caption

_____ 5. The footprints must belong to George.

    ____   ☐   ☐

    Sentence   Picture   Caption

*For more activities like this, please see our *Smarty Pants Puzzles™* series.

Surfing* (pp. 28-29)

(2 pages)

A photo of Charlie starting to carve.

¹Charlie lives in California near the ocean. ²She lives in the house that her dad grew up in. ³When Charlie was five her dad taught her to swim, and later, when she was older, her mom taught her to surf. ⁴Charlie is so good that she places first in many amateur surfing competitions. ⁵She wants to surf professionally someday and be one of the top professional surfers in the world like Stephanie Gilmore, the 2012 Women's World Champion from Australia. ⁶Surfing isn't as easy as it looks. ⁷It takes a lot of strength, endurance, and balance to be very good, especially as a professional surfer. ⁸Sometimes big waves knock Charlie off her board, but she always goes back out for another wave. ⁹Surfing also takes a lot of practice such as learning how to carve, or turn on a wave; how to cutback, which means reversing direction; or ride the barrel, which means surfing inside the barrel (tube) of the wave, but Charlie loves it. ¹⁰When the waves are good, then it's cranking!

*For more activities like this, please see our *Smarty Pants Puzzles*™ series.

Assume all the statements and facts in the puzzles are true. Select the best answer, a-e, for each statement. Then write the sentence number(s) and/or check the box that provides the best evidence for answers a–d.
- a. This is true.
- b. This is probably true but might be false.
- c. This is false.
- d. This is probably false but might be true.
- e. None of the above. There is not enough evidence.

_____ 1. Some of the top professional surfers in the world are women.

_____ ☐ ☐
Sentence Picture Caption

_____ 2. Charlie's dad also surfs.

____ ____ ☐ ☐
Sentences Picture Caption

_____ 3. Unlike other sports, surfing doesn't require practice to be good.

____ ____ ☐ ☐
Sentences Picture Caption

_____ 4. Charlie inherited her talent for surfing from her mom.

____ ☐ ☐
Sentence Picture Caption

_____ 5. Charlie never does any type of strength or endurance training.

____ ____ ____ ☐ ☐
Sentences Picture Caption

_____ 6. The photo shows Charlie reversing direction.

____ ☐ ☐
Sentence Picture Caption

2.3 Classroom Quickies™* (p. 30)

Quotation

Use the letters underneath to fill in the chart so that words are formed and the quotation makes sense. A shaded space in the chart shows the end of a word. (The end of a line in the chart is not necessarily the end of a word.)

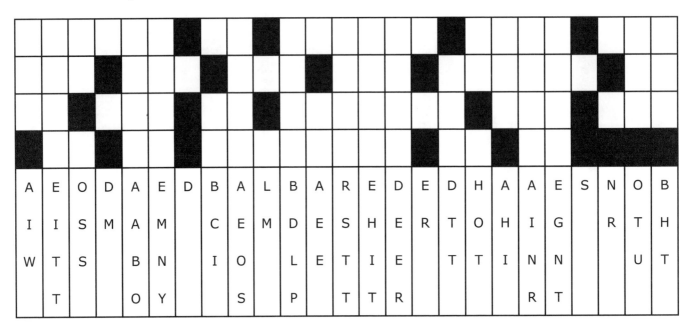

Squares

How many squares are here?

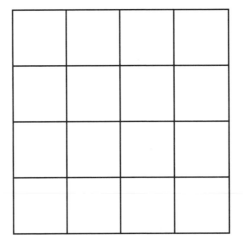

*For more activities like this, please see our *Classroom Quickies™* series.

2.4 Seven Chairs (p. 31)

Three women each have two daughters.

They are having lunch at a restaurant.

There are only seven chairs in the restaurant.

All the women are seated.

How is this possible?

How this is possible: _____

_____

_____

_____

2.5 Dr. Funster's Visual Mind Benders®*

Activity Description

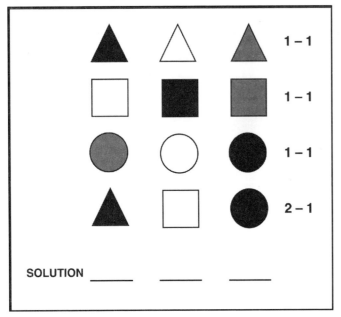

The first number in each row tells the number of figures from that row that will appear in the solution. The second number tells how many of the figures in the row are in the same position in the solution as they are in the row. Each solution will have one of each shape, so in this example, one triangle, one square, and one circle.

Hints

1. You may cut out the figures found on page 373 and place them in the solution spots as you try different possibilities.

2. You may find it helpful to cover up the eliminated figures in the first three rows as you try each solution. Do this by placing the matching cutout over each figure as it is eliminated. These are easy to pick up if your trial solution does not check out.

3. Each problem has one and only one possible solution.

4. Each solution must contain one of each shape—one triangle, one square, one circle, and one hexagon. There is no restriction as to pattern.

5. Students and teachers may arrive at different methods of solution. The only restriction is that the solution must check out with the clues at the end of each row.

Sample Problem

SOLUTION

The numbers at the end of Row 4 tell you that two figures from that row must appear in the solution. One of these two will be in the same position in the solution as it is in Row 4. From Rows 1 and 3 you can tell that it could be either the ▲ or the ●, since they are in the same position in these rows as they are in Row 4.

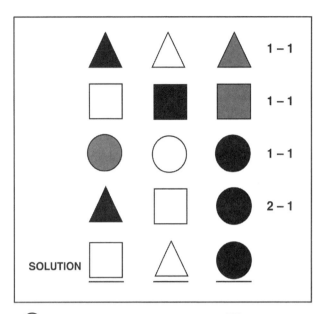

FIRST POSSIBILITY

If you try the ▲ in the first position, then no other triangle can be used. (The first number at the end of Row 1 tells you that only one triangle is used.) If the ▲ is in the first position, then none of the other figures in the first position can be used since the figures from Rows 2 and 3 must appear in their same position. This eliminates the □ and the ●. (That also means that the □ cannot be used in the second position because Row 4 uses only one figure in the same position.)

The second position must be occupied by either the ■ or the ○. (They are in the second position in their rows and must, according to the second number at the end of the row, be in that position if they are in the solution.) If you try the ■ in position two, then you cannot use any other square, and the ○ is eliminated.

This leaves only the ● for position three.

You now have a possible solution. Check your answer against the number clues at the end of each row.

- Do you have one triangle in the same position? (Yes.)
- Do you have one square in the same position? (Yes.)
- Do you have one circle in the same position? (Yes.)
- Do you have two figures from Row 4? (Yes.)
- Is one (and only one) figure from Row 4 in the same position? (Oops—No!)

This solution does not work. Review your choices above and try some alternatives.

SECOND POSSIBILITY

Leaving the ▲ in position one, try the ○ in position two and the ■ in position three. Checking this answer against the clues given at the ends of the rows, you see that you do have one figure from each of the first three rows in the same position. You do not, however, have two figures from Row 4. This solution does not work either. Try again.

THIRD POSSIBILITY

Place the ● in position three. With the ● in the third position, the possible figures for position one are the ▲ and the □. You know from your first two tries, however, that the ▲ cannot be in position one. This means that the □ must be there. This leaves only position two open, and it must be filled with a triangle. The only triangle that can go in position two is the white one. Third solution, therefore, is □, △, ●. Check your answer again. If the answer to each question is yes, you have the correct solution.

2.5 Dr. Funster's Visual Mind Benders®

Solution figures

Cut out the figures below to help you solve the Visual Mind Benders problems on pages 34 and 35.

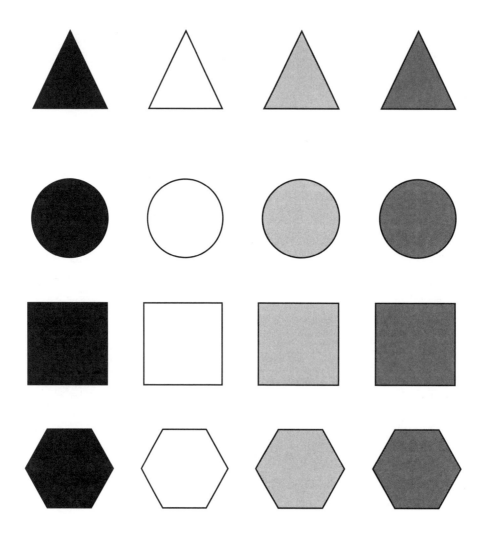

Dr. Funster's Visual Mind Benders®* (p. 34)

1.

1 – 1
One of the triangles is in the solution, and it is in the same location.

1 – 1
One of the squares is in the solution, and it is in the same location.

1 – 1
One of the circles is in the solution, and it is in the same location.

1 – 0
One of the hexagons is in the solution but not in the same location.

2 – 1
Two of the figures are in the solution, but only one is in the same location.

2 – 1
Two of the figures are in the solution, but only one is in the same location.

2 – 0
Two of the figures are in the solution, and neither is in the same location.

SOLUTION

_____   _____   _____   _____

*For more activities like this, please see our *Dr. Funster's Visual Mind Benders*® series.

Dr. Funster's Visual Mind Benders®* (p. 35)

2.

1 – 0
One of the triangles is in the solution but not in the same location.

1 – 1
One of the squares is in the solution, and it is in the same location.

1 – 0
One of the circles is in the solution but not in the same location.

1 – 0
One of the hexagons is in the solution but not in the same location.

2 – 1
Two of the figures are in the solution, but only one is in the same location.

2 – 1
Two of the figures are in the solution, but only one is in the same location.

2 – 1
Two of the figures are in the solution, but only one is in the same location.

SOLUTION

_____   _____   _____   _____

*For more activities like this, please see our *Dr. Funster's Visual Mind Benders®* series.

2.6 Mind Benders®*

How to Solve a Multi-Dimensional Mind Bender®

A *Mind Benders®* problem gives you information and asks you to match one set to the other. You can solve the problem by reading and analyzing the clues. Be sure to fill in the entire chart with true (+) or false (-). The sample problem below takes you through the steps.

Sample Problem

Jim, Jason, and Tom have last names Smith, Lyons, and Dutcher. Each boy has a favorite sport (soccer, tennis, and fishing). Read the clues to find each boy's last name and favorite sport.

1. Jason plays his favorite sport by himself, but also plays Dutcher's favorite sport, tennis.

2. Lyons knows Tom and Smith, but he doesn't play any of the sports they play.

	Smith	Lyons	Dutcher	soccer	tennis	fishing
Jim						
Jason						
Tom						
soccer			
tennis			
fishing			

*For more activities like this, please see our *Mind Benders®* series.

Clue 1 tells us that Dutcher's favorite sport is tennis and Jason's last name is not Dutcher. Mark all these answers on the chart (1a).

Clue 1 also tells us Jason plays his favorite sport by himself. Since tennis and soccer require other players, Jason's favorite sport must be fishing. Mark all these answers on the chart (1b).

Clue 2 tells us that Lyons knows Tom and Smith so Tom's last name is not Lyons or Smith so it is Dutcher. Mark these answers on the chart (2a).

	Smith	Lyons	Dutcher	soccer	tennis	fishing
Jim			.			1b −
Jason			1a −	1b −	1b −	1b +
Tom						1b −
soccer			1a −			
tennis	1a −	1a −	1a +			
fishing			1a −			

Since Clue 2 tells us that Lyons doesn't play any of the sports the other two play and Clue 1 tells us that Dutcher and Jason both play tennis and Jason's favorite sport is fishing, then Lyons cannot play tennis, fish, or be named Jason. So, we now know that Lyons is named Jim and plays soccer. This leaves us with Jason's last name as Smith. We now know everyone's first and last names as well as each person's favorite sport. Mark these answers on the chart (2b).

Tom Dutcher's favorite sport is tennis, Jim Lyons' favorite sport is soccer, and Jason Smith's favorite sport is fishing.

	Smith	Lyons	Dutcher	soccer	tennis	fishing
Jim	2b −	2b +	2a −	2b +	2b −	1b −
Jason	2b +	2b −	1a −	1b −	1b −	1b +
Tom	2a −	2a −	2a +	2b −	2b +	1b −
soccer	2b −	2b +	1a −			
tennis	1a −	1a −	1a +			
fishing	2b +	2b −	1a −			

2.6 Mind Benders®

Class President*   (p. 38)

Agnes, Betsy, Cornelius, and Dexter each voted for a different person for class president (Grant, Houh, McGuire, and Sterling). Read the clues to find who each student voted for.

1. The boy who voted for McGuire is older than the person who voted for Sterling and is younger than Dexter.

2. The person who voted for Houh is taller than Betsy and the person who voted for Grant.

3. Agnes didn't vote for Houh.

	Grant	Houh	McGuire	Sterling
Agnes				
Betsy				
Cornelius				
Dexter				

*For more activities like this, please see our *Mind Benders*® series.

Part-Time Jobs* (p. 39)

Jeanette, Marcia, Saralee, and Theodora all hold part-time jobs after school. The jobs are carpenter's apprentice, cook, delivery person for a pizzeria, and paper route. Each person uses part of her earnings to pay for a cell phone. The cell phone colors are blue, green, red, and white. Read the clues to find each girl's job and cell phone color.

1. The carpenter's apprentice and the person with the white cell phone live on a street which is two blocks away from the street where Saralee and the person with the green cell phone live.

2. Jeanette and the cook live next door to each other, but Marcia and the delivery person live two doors away from each other.

3. Theodora lives on the same street as the person with the red cell phone.

4. The cook does not have the white cell phone.

	carpenter's apprentice	cook	delivery person	paper route	blue	green	red	white
Jeanette								
Marcia								
Saralee								
Theodora								
blue								
green								
red								
white								

*For more activities like this, please see our *Mind Benders*® series.

Pet Cats* (pp. 40-41)

(2 pages)

Abner, Crystal, Edmund, and Joy, whose last names are Dinton, Harmon, Landon, and Magland, each have a cat. The colors of the cats are black, gray, white, and yellow, and the cats' names are Fluffy, Kitty, Pretty, and Sleepy. Read the clues to find each person's full name and the name and color of their cat.

1. Magland has the yellow cat.

2. Sleepy's owner, who is neither Joy nor Harmon, does not have the gray cat.

3. Abner's and Landon's cats are short-haired, while Crystal's and Dinton's cats are long-haired.

4. Neither Pretty nor the gray cat, which are short-haired, is owned by Edmund.

5. Crystal's cat, which is not white or yellow, is not Fluffy.

*For more activities like this, please see our *Mind Benders*® series.

	Dinton	Harmon	Landon	Magland	black	gray	white	yellow	Fluffy	Kitty	Pretty	Sleepy
Abner												
Crystal												
Edmund												
Joy												
black												
gray												
white												
yellow												
Fluffy												
Kitty												
Pretty												
Sleepy												

Important Takeaways

Three important takeaways that I want to remember from this chapter are:

1. _____

   _____

   _____

2. _____

   _____

   _____

3. _____

   _____

   _____

IMPORTANT

3.1 My CT Toolbox

Toolbox Thought Experiment (p. 44): Based on what you already know about critical thinking and how it relates to your own life, what kind of tools do you want to make sure get added? What would their function be? It's okay to make up your own names for these tools, but be as precise as you can in describing how they would function in terms of helping you with your critical thinking.

_____

_____

_____

_____

_____

3.2 Facts vs. Opinions

⭐ **Student Poll** (p. 45):   Place a check mark next to the places where you encounter facts and opinions.

Place	Facts	Opinions
School	_____	_____
Online	_____	_____
Books	_____	_____
Advertising	_____	_____
Texting	_____	_____
Conversations	_____	_____
Movies	_____	_____
Arguments	_____	_____
Blogs	_____	_____
TV	_____	_____
Lyrics	_____	_____

Looking at your list, are facts and opinions found in different places? Are there some places where you are more likely to find one more often than the other?

Definitions of Fact and Opinion (p.45)

Take a stab at defining a "fact":

_____

Give a go now with "opinion":

_____

My Prediction (p. 46)

I think you'll be telling me about _____

_____

Example of an Opinion Using a Signal Word (p. 47)

Here's my example of an opinion using a signal word:

_____

_____

⭐ Student Poll (p. 48)

> Your friend says to you: "Recent comments made by Dr. Sam George
>
> prove that most patients would opt for less aggressive treatment for
>
> back pain if they were informed of all the risks and benefits for all
>
> treatment options."

This is an example of _____ a fact _____ an opinion.

I made my choice because _____

_____

Fact or Opinion? Practice (p. 50):   Check whether these statements are facts or opinions. You are not concerned with whether the facts are true or not.

1. In 2012, 64.6% of married women in the United States were employed.

    _____ Fact   _____ Opinion

2. Mayor Marks doesn't have a clue as to how to solve the housing shortage in the city.

    _____ Fact   _____ Opinion

3. The amount that the Tooth Fairy is paying out on a tooth is surging due to the improvement in the economy, because parents believe they can afford it, and because it is hard for them to say no to their kids.

    _____ Fact   _____ Opinion

4. Some grade schools now provide iPads for use in the classroom.

    _____ Fact   _____ Opinion

5. I don't feel sorry for the auto industry. U.S. auto manufacturers are having it great right now. They are making fistfuls of dollars—more than they have ever made.

    _____ Fact   _____ Opinion

⭐ **Student Poll** (p. 50):   Read this true story from the October 2013 *Reader's Digest*:

> On my way home from my mother's, I realized I'd left my cell phone at
>
> her house, so I went back to get it. Upon retrieving it, I noticed I had
>
> a message from Mom. She'd texted, "You left your phone."

On a scale from 1 ("Terrible!") to 10 ("Perfect!"), rate the critical thinking skills going on in this story by the mother. _____

3.3 Possible, Probable, and Proven

***Star Trek* Thought Experiment** (p. 51): You and your friends have just seen the new *Star Trek* movie, and while eating a pepperoni and extra cheese pizza, one of your friends asks you if you think there really are aliens living on other planets.

What would you say?

_____

_____

_____

_____

Based on your answer, on a scale from 1 is ("No way!") to 10 ("Definitely!"), rate the following statements.

_____ It is possible that there is life beyond our solar system.

_____ It is probable that there is life beyond our solar system.

_____ It has been proven that there is life beyond our solar system—after all aliens were found in the spaceship in Roswell!

Do you need to revise your prediction? If so, do it here. (p. 51)

_____

_____

Possible? Probable? Proven? Practice (p. 53): For each of the statements, check if you think it is possible, probable, proven, or none, and then you need to explain why.

Note: "None" means that due to our understanding of reality, it is either impossible or so improbable that it does not even meet the threshold of possible.

1. Bigfoot exists.

_____ Possible _____ Probable _____ Proven _____ None

_____

_____

2. Mermaids exist.

_____ Possible _____ Probable _____ Proven _____ None

_____

_____

3. Voyager 1 has recorded for the first time ever the sounds in interstellar space.

_____ Possible _____ Probable _____ Proven _____ None

_____

_____

4. There is a type of insect that has interlocking gears that actually work on its hind legs.

_____ Possible _____ Probable _____ Proven _____ None

_____

_____

5. Butterflies in the Amazon drink turtle tears.

_____ Possible _____ Probable _____ Proven _____ None

_____

_____

3.4 Evidence

Did Beth Notsofast Steal the Wallet and the Money? (p. 54)

Did Beth Notsofast steal the wallet and the money?

_____ Yes!   _____ No!   _____ Unknown

Why? Cite your evidence, or explain why you think there is a lack of evidence.

_____

_____

_____

_____

_____

Case of the Missing Wallet (pp. 56-57): Let's look at the evidence in our case.   (2 pages)

Judy's Conclusion: _____

Evidence #1:   Judy passed Beth coming out of the locker room when she (Judy) entered it after
                practice.

Does this evidence prove that Beth stole the wallet?

_____ Yes   _____ No   _____ Maybe

Why? _____

_____

Evidence #2:   No one else was in the locker room when Judy looked around after she found her
                locker wide open and after Beth had left.

Does this evidence prove that Beth stole the wallet?

_____ Yes   _____ No   _____ Maybe

Why? _____

_____

<u>Evidence #3</u>:   Beth wouldn't look Judy in the eye or say "hi," even though Judy feels she is a "really
        good friend."

Does this evidence prove that Beth stole the wallet?

_____ Yes   _____ No   _____ Maybe

Why? _____

_____

<u>Evidence #4</u>:   Judy's locker was wide open when she came back to the locker room, but it had been
        shut and locked when Judy left the locker room.

Does this evidence prove that Beth stole the wallet?

_____ Yes   _____ No   _____ Maybe

Why? _____

_____

Total # of: _____ Yes   _____ No   _____ Maybe

4 Yes answers =   You think the evidence is conclusive.

4 No answers =   You think the evidence is definitely not conclusive.

4 Maybe answers =   You think there is some probability that she did it, but not enough to be
               convinced.

Mix of answers: You are not convinced by the evidence, though you may find some of it
               convincing or not convincing.

If you feel certain that Beth stole the wallet, what type of evidence might shake that certainty? If
you don't feel certain that Beth stole the wallet, what type of evidence would you need in order to be
convinced?

_____

_____

_____

Check-in (p. 58): On a scale from 1 ("No way!") to 10 ("I've got this!"), rate your confidence in understanding what evidence is and how to evaluate it.

_____ I understand what evidence is.

_____ I understand how to evaluate evidence.

If your score is below 10 on either of these statements, then what do you need to ask your teacher or one of the other students in class in order to make your confidence a 10? When you're ready, take the quiz.

_____

_____

The Evidence in Arguments Quiz (p. 58): Answer the following questions the best you can. If you get stuck, then sneak a peak. When you're done, go back and check your answers. If you need some additional help understanding evidence, then ask your teacher or another student to coach you.

1. The reasons in an argument are the _____.

2. In an argument, evidence either _____ the conclusion or it doesn't.

3. In an argument, evidence is either _____ or _____.

4. Critical thinkers need to know how to evaluate evidence. _____ True _____ False

5. Check the factors we need to consider when we evaluate evidence in arguments.

_____ Kind of evidence   _____ Accuracy of evidence

_____ Relevancy of evidence   _____ If it is direct evidence

_____ If it is indirect evidence   _____ Quality of the evidence

_____ Quantity of evidence   _____ What our gut tells us

3.5 Creativity, Creative Thinking & Creative Problem Solving

⭐ **Student Poll** (p. 59): On a scale from 1 ("I don't think so!") to 10 ("Wow!"), rate how creative you think the woman pictured on page 59 is in trying to solve her problem of knitting a hat.

I give the woman a _____.

If You Needed to Knit a Hat (p. 60)

If you needed to knit a hat, what would you need to consider? (Even if you have never knitted in your life you should be able to figure out some of the things you'd have to consider.)

_____

_____

_____

_____

💡 **My Creative Problem Solving Thought Experiment** (p. 60): Describe a problem that you once had to solve, how you went about finding a solution, and how you finally solved it. Be as specific ajnd concrete as you can.

My problem was: _____

_____

_____

How I went about finding a solution: _____

_____

_____

_____

My solution was: _____

_____

_____

The Incomplete Figure Creativity Practice (p. 61): Using the figure below, give yourself 5 minutes to create something from it.

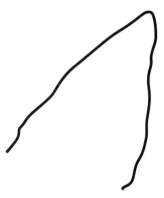

Title: _____

 Nine Dot Thought Experiment (p. 62): Connect all nine dots by drawing only four straight lines with your pen or pencil never leaving the paper.

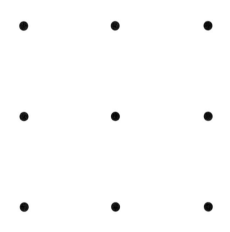

"Aha!" Thought Experiment (p. 63): Describe a time when you had an "aha!" moment—a moment of sudden insight or inspiration.

_____

_____

_____

Inspiration Thought Experiment (p. 63): What triggers inspiration in you? Check all that apply, and then identify your top 3.

_____ Listening to music   _____ Brainstorming

_____ Daydreaming   _____ Getting out in nature

_____ Taking a break   _____ Running, skateboarding etc.

_____ Doing something artistic   _____ Playing a game

_____ Discuss ideas with others   _____ Reading

_____ Experiencing the absurd   _____ Watching a movie

Other: _____

My top 3 are:

1. _____

2. _____

3. _____

Check-in (p. 66): Rate your confidence level about what you've learned in this chapter. Circle the picture that fits. No clue? Ask a friend or your teacher to coach you.

No problem—I'm celebrating!

No clue! I gave up & went to sleep!

Important Takeaways

Three important takeaways that I want to remember from this chapter are:

1. _____

_____

_____

2. _____

_____

_____

3. _____

_____

_____

3.7 Individual Activities

1. **Incomplete Figure** (p. 70)

   Using the figure below, give yourself 5 minutes to create something from it.

Title: _____

2. **Divide the Figure** (p. 70)

   Divide this figure into four equal parts that are the same size and shape.

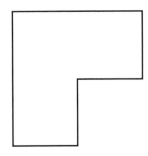

3. **The Candle Problem** (p. 71)

Using the material on the table: a cardboard box of thumbtacks, matches, and a candle, figure out how to attach the candle to the wall above the table so that the wax does not drip on the table.

My solution: _____

_____

_____

3.8 Group Activities & Discussion

7. **The Case of the Lead Masks** (pp. 73-79)   (4 pages)

If the class has not formed detective agencies yet, then have the class divide into pairs of two detectives per agency and have them come up with an agency name. Read through the case notes on pages 74-75 as a class and then have the detectives work through the questions on the next four pages. Put the chart found at the end of this case study on the board, and during the class discussion record their answers on the chart on the board as the class discusses the case study. Discuss the additional questions that the detectives want answered, and then work as a group to come to some consensus about what probably happened to da Cruz and Viana.

A. Evaluating the Evidence (pp. 76-78)

Each detective agency is to answer the following questions that will require them to evaluate evidence. Select the best answer based on the evidence, and then indicate the evidence that supports your answer and note the sentence number.

T = True	PT = Probably True but might be false
F = False	PF = Probably False but might be true

U = Not enough evidence to make a determination.

1. Da Cruz and Viana expected to meet someone.

_____ T   _____ PT   _____ F   _____ PF   _____ U

Evidence: _____

_____

_____

_____

2. Da Cruz and Viana expected to encounter some form of radiation.

_____ T   _____ PT   _____ F   _____ PF   _____ U

Evidence: _____

_____

_____

_____

3. Da Cruz and Viana were conducting an experiment.

_____ T   _____ PT   _____ F   _____ PF   _____ U

Evidence: _____

_____

_____

_____

4. Da Cruz and Viana were in a violent fight with someone.

_____ T   _____ PT   _____ F   _____ PF   _____ U

Evidence: _____

_____

_____

_____

5. Da Cruz and Viana were murdered during a robbery.

_____ T   _____ PT   _____ F   _____ PF   _____ U

Evidence: _____

_____

_____

_____

6. Da Cruz and Viana intentionally killed themselves by ingesting the capsules.

_____ T   _____ PT   _____ F   _____ PF   _____ U

Evidence: _____

_____

_____

_____

7. Da Cruz and Viana expected to meet aliens on Vintém Hill in Niterói.

_____ T   _____ PT   _____ F   _____ PF   _____ U

Evidence: _____

_____

_____

_____

8. Da Cruz and Viana were killed by aliens.

_____ T   _____ PT   _____ F   _____ PF   _____ U

Evidence: _____

_____

_____

_____

B. Working Hypothesis and Line of Inquiry (p. 78)

What is your agency's working hypothesis about what happened to da Cruz and Viana? In other words, you and your partner need to decide what is the most probable explanation for what happened to the two men. You will need to explain your reasoning and the evidence for it. "Unknown" will not be an acceptable answer for this activity.

1. Working hypothesis:

_____

_____

2. Reasoning and Evidence:

_____

_____

_____

_____

_____

_____

3. What additional questions do you want answered? Why?

_____

_____

_____

_____

4.1 Emotional Words and Arguments

⭐ **Student Poll** (p. 80): Rate the following words as Hot (a positive feeling), Cold (a negative feeling), Nada (neutral feeling—nothing much either way) depending on how they make YOU feel.

_____ Final exam	_____ Super Bowl
_____ Dinner	_____ Corrupt
_____ Freedom	_____ Curfew
_____ Opportunity	_____ Honor
_____ Comedian	_____ Traitor
_____ Death	_____ Lazy
_____ Sight	_____ Weight

💡 **Hot, Cold, and Nada Thought Experiment** (p. 81): Select two words from each category and explain briefly why those words felt hot, cold, or neutral to you.

_____ felt Hot because: _____

_____

_____ felt Hot because: _____

_____

_____ felt Cold because: _____

_____

_____ felt Cold because: _____

_____

_____ felt Nada because: _____

_____

_____ felt Nada because: _____

_____

Value Claim Made by Bobby's Dad (p. 82)

"That boy is out of control, he never listens. It is 11:30 p.m., way past his

curfew of 11:00 p.m. It just shows how irresponsible and self-centered he is."

What is the value claim of the emotive statements above made by the Bobby's dad?

_____

⭐ **Student Poll** (p. 82): On a scale from 1 ("Easy!") to 10 ("Really hard!"), rate how easy or hard it was to figure out the value claim. _____

If your rating was a number other than 1 ("Easy"), then select the reason. Select only one answer.

The reason that figuring out the value claim was hard was because of the:

_____ Emotionally charged language   _____ Neutral language

_____ Cognitive meaning of what was said   _____ Other: _____

My Prediction (p. 83)

Having escaped immediate permanent incapacitation, the turkeys were overjoyed!

I think you'll be telling me about _____

_____

Emotionally Charged Language Practice I (p. 84): List the emotionally charged words in the argument below about the lyrics of rock music:

> The lyrics of rock music today are filthy and immoral. They alone will cause our
>
> society to fall into ruin. So we must ban all rock music.

_____

Emotionally Charged Language Practice II (pp. 84-85): Answer "Yes" or "No" for the questions below, which relate to the rock music argument.

1. _____ The lyrics of ALL rock music are "filthy and immoral."

2. _____ The lyrics of rock music, by themselves, will lead to the ruin of society.

3. _____ The argument provides evidence which actually supports the conclusion that all rock music must be banned.

4. _____ My emotions got engaged either for or against the conclusion.

The cognitive meaning of this argument is (use neutral language not emotionally charged language):

_____

_____

The value claim is: _____

Neutral Words Practice (pp. 85-86): Restate each statement using only neutral words and phrases. Make sure you keep the same meaning.

1. Sam thinks he's another Einstein.

    _____

2. That girl is so nosy.

    _____

3. Mr. Jeffers really raked me over the coals because I didn't do my homework.

    _____

4. My brother is so pig-headed.

    _____

5. The Seattle Mariners are a worthless, lazy baseball team who waste the fans' hard-earned money.

    _____

    _____

Neutral Language & Arguments Practice (p. 86): Restate each argument using neutral language, but keep the same meaning. Don't worry about whether it is a good argument or not.

Tip: Read through the argument and make sure you understand it. Then work with each statement found in the argument. When you are done, read through the argument again to make sure you kept the same meaning.

1. The lottery should be abolished. It steals food right out of the mouth of children and robs families of money that they need in order to pay their mortgage and utilities.

   _____

   _____

   _____

2. If you are against cloning organs, then you are against saving lives. Only someone who is selfish and cruel would deny people the right to save their lives, so support giving research grants for cloning organs.

   _____

   _____

   _____

   _____

3. Judy, you need to dump Charlie. He's nothing but a selfish, two-timing boyfriend who doesn't really love you at all.

   _____

   _____

Value Claim Identification Practice (p. 87):   State the value claims for each of the three arguments above.

1. _____

2. _____

3. _____

Check-in (p. 87):   Rate your confidence level regarding your ability to identify the value claim being made in an argument.   Circle the picture that fits.   No clue how to identify the value claim?   Ask a friend or your teacher to coach you.

Feeling good!

No clue! This stuff is kryptonite!!

4.2 The Problem with Ambiguity

The "Why" of Understanding Language Practice (p. 88)

On the placard held by the frog, list, as concisely as you can, the reasons why understanding language is important for us as critical thinkers. If you have forgotten or are unsure, then review 4.1.

The "Say What?" Thought Experiment (p. 89): Ever find yourself saying, "Say what?"—meaning "What did you say? I don't get it"—after someone said something to you? This Thought Experiment is going to get you thinking about how language can be troublesome and even defective. For each of the words below, provide at least two different meanings.

1. pen _____

2. bank _____

3. suit _____

4. hard _____

5. critical _____

6. race _____

Two Different Meanings of "Visiting Relatives Can Be Boring." (p. 90)
Here's another statement: "Visiting relatives can be boring." What do you think is meant here? See if you can provide two different meanings for this statement.

1. _____

2. _____

Do you need to revise your prediction? If so, do it here. (p. 90)

_____

_____

Ambiguity in Statements (p. 91)

Bracket the two meanings in Examples 2 and 3, and then provide the meaning of each statement.

Example 2:

a. Milk drinkers are turning to powder.

Meaning: _____

_____

b. Milk drinkers are turning to powder.

Meaning: _____

_____

Example 3:

a. Enraged cow injures farmer with ax.

Meaning: _____

_____

b. Enraged cow injures farmer with ax.

Meaning: _____

_____

Ambiguity and Real-Life Headlines Practice (p. 93): These headlines are not made up; they are real! Provide two alternate meanings for each headline. Then choose the one that you think is the most probable and explain why.

1. Bill Would Permit Ads On Eyeglasses

    a. _____

    b. _____

    My choice: _____ because _____

    _____

2. Chef Throws His Heart Into Helping Feed Needy

    a. _____

    b. _____

    My choice: _____ because _____

    _____

3. Stolen Painting Found By Tree

    a. _____

    b. _____

    My choice: _____ because _____

    _____

4. Man Eating Piranha Mistakenly Sold As Pet Fish

    a. _____

    b. _____

    My choice: _____ because _____

    _____

4.3 Vagueness

The Broccoli Thought Experiment (p. 94): If you were a child who wasn't too keen on eating broccoli and your mother said to you "You can have dessert if you eat a little more broccoli," how much broccoli would you actually have to eat to get your dessert?

_____

_____

Do you think you and your mother would have the same understanding about what a "little more broccoli" would mean? Why or why not?

_____

_____

_____

Student Poll (p. 95): Who is rich? Check the boxes that you feel apply. Unsure, then put a question mark. When you are done, poll two other people by asking them the question and the choices, marking their choices on the other spaces.

Someone is rich who makes:

$1,000,000 a year	_____	_____	_____
$400,000 a year	_____	_____	_____
$250,000 a year	_____	_____	_____
$100,000 a year	_____	_____	_____
$50,000 a year	_____	_____	_____
$10,000 a year	_____	_____	_____

Reason for Different Answers (p. 95)

When you compare your answers to those of the other people you polled, did you see any different answers? If you did, why do you think this happened?

_____

_____

Writing a Law (p. 95)

What if we were writing a law and it would apply specifically to people who were rich, what would we need to do to avoid this confusion?

_____

_____

(2 pages)

Vagueness Practice (pp. 97-98):   Decide if the following statements are vague or not. If they are vague, identify the vague word or phrase and explain what you would need to know in order for the statements not to be vague. If they are not vague, then point out what makes them not vague.

1. There are loads of people at the soccer game.

    Vague _____   Vague term/phrase: _____

    Not Vague _____

    _____

    _____

2. Oregon became a state in 1859.

    Vague _____   Vague term/phrase: _____

    Not Vague _____

    _____

    _____

3. I'm more or less done with my homework.

    Vague _____   Vague term/phrase: _____

    Not Vague _____

    _____

    _____

4. I think paying $100 for jeans is excessive.

Vague _____ Vague term/phrase: _____

Not Vague _____

_____

_____

5. Ad: "Use L'été by La Femme for skin like peaches and cream."

Vague _____ Vague term/phrase: _____

Not Vague _____

_____

_____

6. Danica Patrick is an inspiration because she is the first female to win a pole position in a NASCAR race, leading the Daytona 500 field, and because she was a contender for the Sprint Cup Rookie of the Year.

Vague _____ Vague term/phrase: _____

Not Vague _____

_____

_____

4.4 Doublespeak: Euphemism & Jargon

 Doublespeak Thought Experiment (p. 99): Match the terms with their definitions, and check your answers once you are done.

<u>Terms</u>   <u>Definitions</u>

_____ 1. political credibility problem   a. receptionist

_____ 2. temporarily displaced inventory   b. plastic trash bag

_____ 3. encore telecast   c. hungry

_____ 4. uninstalled   d. stolen goods

_____ 5. exceed the odor threshold   e. a lie

_____ 6. director of first impressions   f. dead civilians

_____ 7. collateral damage   g. death

_____ 8. immediate permanent incapacitation   h. rerun

_____ 9. waste management bag   i. fired

_____ 10. food insecure   j. stink

Food Insercurity Questions (p. 101)

By Ned Resnikoff   Millions of Americans fell victim to food insecurity when the Great
                             Recession hit in 2009, but didn't benefit from the economic recovery. And
                             the worst may be yet to come. **read story**

How would the term "food insecurity" make you feel about these Americans and what they might be facing in the future?

_____

_____

If, however, the caption had said:

> Millions of Americans fell victim to hunger when the Great Recession hit in 2009, but
>
> didn't benefit from the economic recovery. And the worst may be yet to come.

Would you feel differently about what happened to millions of Americans? Would it make you think differently about "the worst" that might happen to them? Are we talking about starvation?

_____

_____

⭐ **Student Poll** (p. 102): Check all the words or phrases that you have heard used to talk about death.

_____ Passed away   _____ Passed over

_____ Put to sleep   _____ Deceased

_____ Gone to a better place   _____ Bought the farm

_____ Gone to meet their maker   _____ In heaven now

_____ Gave up the ghost   _____ With the angels

(2 pages)

Doublespeak Practice (pp. 104-105): For each pair of statements, explain whether or not they have the same emotional impact on you and why. Underline the euphemism.

1. a. My father was recently uninstalled from his job.

    b. My father was recently fired from his job.

    _____

    _____

2. a. We had to bury the decommissioned aggressor quantum killed in the battle.

    b. We had to bury the dead enemy soldiers killed in the battle.

    _____

    _____

3. a. Everyone is upset with the tax increase that was passed.

    b. Everyone is upset with the revenue enhancement that was passed.

    _____

    _____

4. a. I can't afford a new car, so I have to buy a used one.

   b. I can't afford a new car, so I have to buy a previously distinguished one.

   _____

   _____

5. a. My cat, Charlie, is experiencing terminal living.

   b. My cat, Charlie, is dying.

   _____

   _____

6. a. I am so tired of the reruns of "The Big Bang Theory."

   b. I am so tired of the encore telecasts of "The Big Bang Theory."

   _____

   _____

4.5 Doublespeak: Gobbledygook & Inflated Language

Gobbledygook Thought Experiment (p. 106): Translate the sentence below to the best of your ability.

"It is a tricky problem to find the particular calibration in timing that would be appropriate to stem the acceleration in risk premiums created by falling incomes without prematurely aborting the decline in the inflation-generated risk premiums."

_____

_____

_____

_____

Your Turn Thought Experiment (p. 108): Now it's your turn to try your hand at gobbledygook. Turn the following sentence into the best, most delicious form of gobbledygook you can!

Students are not allowed to have hot drinks in the classroom.

_____

_____

_____

Student Poll (p. 108): Check the box that you think best explains the following terms.

1. pupil stations

    _____ Classrooms   _____ Desks   _____ Lockers

2. career associate scanning professionals

    _____ X-ray technician   _____ Librarian   _____ Grocery store checkout clerks

3. reutilization marketing yard

    _____ Flea market   _____ Discount store   _____ Junkyard

4. vertical transportation corps

    _____ Astronauts   _____ Elevator operators   _____ Mountain climbing guides

The "I Spy" Thought Experiment (p. 110): Like the children's game that says "I spy with my little eye," what can we do to "spy," or see, doublespeak? In other words, what can we do as critical thinkers to recognize it, not be taken in by it, and figure out why it is being used?

I can _____

_____

_____

_____

Now come up with an idea for a commercial, or a public service announcement (PSA), to help other teens and young adults understand what doublespeak is and what they can do to not be taken in by it.

My PSA idea: _____

_____

_____

_____

_____

⭐ **Student Poll** (p. 110): From the Reader's Digest website:

> My neighbor, a police officer, pulled someone over
>
> for texting while driving, a big no-no in our state.
>
> The driver was having none of it.
>
> "I was not texting!" she insisted indignantly.
>
> "I was on Facebook."

On a scale from 1 ("Lame!") to 10 ("Crazy hot!"), rate the critical thinking skills going on in this story by the driver. _____

Important Takeaways

Three important takeaways that I want to remember from this chapter are:

1. _____

   _____

   _____

2. _____

   _____

   _____

3. _____

   _____

   _____

4.7 Individual Activities

1. **Using Neutral Language** (p. 114)
   Restate each argument using neutral language and keep the same meaning. Don't worry if it is a good argument or not. Then state the value claim(s) for each argument.

   a. Those disgusting, horrid video games cause an increase in the violent behavior of our young people. It's this barbaric behavior that leads to murder and mayhem. I say we should ban children under the age of eighteen from buying or playing these wretched video games.

   Argument: _____

   _____

   _____

   _____

   Value claim: _____

   b. Bootleg music CDs should be legal because the artists are greedy multimillionaires who rip-off hard working adults and kids who don't have a lot of spending money. Besides it means less pollution because there will be less CDs tossed in the dump.

   Argument: _____

   _____

   _____

   _____

   Value claim: _____

2. **Testing for Ambiguity and Vagueness** (p. 115)

Decide if there is a problem in the following statements or headlines. If there is, then indicate whether the problem in each statement, headline, or ad is due to ambiguity or being vague, and then identify the problem word or phrase.

a. A majority of the 270 electoral votes is required to elect the President of the United States of America.

_____ No problem _____ Problem _____ Ambiguity _____ Vague

Problem word or phrase: _____

b. Everyone in Congress is rich.

_____ No problem _____ Problem _____ Ambiguity _____ Vague

Problem word or phrase: _____

c. Headline: USPS POSTS $5 BILLION LOSS

_____ No problem _____ Problem _____ Ambiguity _____ Vague

Problem word or phrase: _____

d. Headline: LACK OF BRAINS HINDERS RESEARCH

_____ No problem _____ Problem _____ Ambiguity _____ Vague

Problem word or phrase: _____

e. Ad: Dog for sale. Eats anything and is especially fond of children.

_____ No problem _____ Problem _____ Ambiguity _____ Vague

Problem word or phrase: _____

f. "I think that Maria spends an excessive amount of time texting her friends!"

_____ No problem _____ Problem _____ Ambiguity _____ Vague

Problem word or phrase: _____

3. **Headlines** (p. 116)

Provide two alternate meanings for each headline. Then choose the one that you think is the most probable and explain why.

a.

Lawyers back despite use of bug spray

By Winda Benedetti
Staff writer

COEUR d'ALENE — The yellow jackets were gone and the pesticide smell was fading but the headaches remained as lawyers returned to the Kootenai County Prosecutor's office

i. _____

ii. _____

My choice: _____ because _____

_____

b.

▶Thailand: Police seize 14 elephants with fake IDs

Thai police said they seized more than a dozen elephants Wednesday in raids after busting a gang that allegedly provided

i. _____

ii. _____

My choice: _____ because _____

_____

4. **Name the Doublespeak** (p. 117)
   Indicate whether the italicized word(s) or phrase is an example of euphemism, jargon, or inflated language.

   a. Teachers are *classroom facilitators*.

   _____ Euphemism   _____ Jargon   _____ Inflated language

   b. In every war there is considerable *collateral damage*.

   _____ Euphemism   _____ Jargon   _____ Inflated language

   c. My mom went to *the powder room*.

   _____ Euphemism   _____ Jargon   _____ Inflated language

   d. "All systems are go and we have *lift off*."

   _____ Euphemism   _____ Jargon   _____ Inflated language

   e. Sam: "What did the officer mean when she radioed '*Taking a code 7*'?"

   _____ Euphemism   _____ Jargon   _____ Inflated language

   f. Customer: "Where will I find *emergency exit lights*?"
       Clerk: "Oh, flashlights are on aisle seven."

   _____ Euphemism   _____ Jargon   _____ Inflated language

5.1 What's Up With Arguments?

⭐ **Student Poll** (p. 120): Where have you encountered arguments? Check all the people or groups of people you have heard make an argument or who tried to persuade you or someone else about something.

_____ Parent(s)	_____ Brother(s)	_____ Sister(s)
_____ Best friend	_____ Team members	_____ Coach
_____ Politicians	_____ School board	_____ Advertisers
_____ People promoting a cause	_____ Student council	_____ Teacher

Did we leave out someone very important from this list? How about YOU? _____

Now on a scale from 1 ("Rarely!") to 10 ("Daily!"), rate how often you make an argument in order to persuade someone about something. _____

Of Monsters and Men Practice (p. 121): Take a closer look at Scott's argument.

> I should be allowed to go with my friends Kevin and Greg to see Of Monsters and Men
>
> since I'm 17 years old and very responsible. I've never missed my curfew or gotten into
>
> trouble and neither has Kevin or Greg. Besides I've kept up my grades all semester.

What is he trying to persuade his parents to allow him to do? This is the conclusion of his argument:

_____

What are the reasons, or evidence, he gives to parents for why he should be allowed to go the concert? These are premises of his argument. There are three premises.

1. _____

2. _____

_____

3. _____

5.2 What Is an Argument?

Two Kinds of Statements That Make Up an Argument (p. 122)

Based on the Of Monsters and Men Argument Practice from section 5.1, what do you think are the two kinds of statements that make up an argument?

_____   _____

Operator and Assertion Practice (p. 124): Working with the second premise of Scott's argument answer the following questions.

1. The two operators are: _____   _____

2. There are how many assertions in the premise? _____

3. Those assertions are:

_____

_____

_____

More Argument Practice (p. 124): Look at the argument Scott's friend Kevin makes about indie folk music and identify the conclusion and the two premises.

> Indie folk music is the best! The artists don't sell out—they're an independent
>
> rock community. They also combine folk music and classic country music with
>
> indie rock to create a unique sound.

Conclusion: _____

Premise 1: _____

_____

Premise 2: _____

_____

My Prediction (p. 125)

I think you will be telling me about _____

_____

Your Argument Thought Experiment (p. 126): Think about an argument you made to someone recently. Identify what was the conclusion of your argument, and then identify the premises, or reasons, for your conclusion—listing each one on a separate line and numbering them. You will get to evaluate your argument later in the chapter.

My conclusion: _____

My premise(s):

_____

_____

_____

_____

 Statement Practice (p. 127): Circle the numbers of the sentences that are statements.

1. It is raining outside.

2. Wilma Rudolph was the first American woman to win three gold medals at a single Olympics.

3. Don't eat cake before dinner.

4. Wow!

5. Amelia Earhart was the first person to fly solo across both the Atlantic and the Pacific oceans.

6. Hillary Clinton was the first U.S. woman in space.

7. Let's go to the beach.

8. Neil Armstrong was the first man to walk on the moon.

9. I suggest you study fractions again before the test Monday.

10. Marie Curie received the Nobel Prize in Physics in 1903 and in Chemistry in 1911.

11. Mr. Spock is half-human and half-Vulcan.

Conclusion Practice (pp. 127-128): In the following problems underline the conclusion. Then circle any indicator words in the sentence and identify whether they are premise indicators or conclusion indicators.

1. All flowers are pretty and a rose is a flower, so a rose must be pretty.

    _____ Premise indicator   _____ Conclusion indicator

2. A rhinoceros is not a vegetable because a rhinoceros is an animal and no animal is a vegetable.

    _____ Premise indicator   _____ Conclusion indicator

3. A crow is black and a raven is black. Both crows and ravens are birds. Therefore, all birds must be black.

    _____ Premise indicator   _____ Conclusion indicator

4. You cannot step twice in the same river, for other waters are ever flowing on to you.

    _____ Premise indicator   _____ Conclusion indicator

5. If Mr. Ed is a horse, then Mr. Ed is a mammal. Mr. Ed is a horse. Hence Mr. Ed is a mammal.

    _____ Premise indicator   _____ Conclusion indicator

6. Since most famous singers are millionaires, and Beyoncé is a famous singer; Beyoncé is probably a millionaire.

    _____ Premise indicator   _____ Conclusion indicator

7. Some girls play ice hockey. Ice hockey is a sport. Therefore, some girls play sports.

    _____ Premise indicator   _____ Conclusion indicator

8. Dogs aren't as smart as cats. My cat can open the pantry door and help herself to the dry cat food stored there. My dog, however, can't figure out how to open the pantry door, and even after the cat opens the door, he can't figure out how to get to the dry cat food.

    _____ Premise indicator   _____ Conclusion indicator

9. Everyone uses the computer these days, and most people have a smart phone. Books are readily available online or as eBooks. Consequently, we should quit publishing books.

    _____ Premise indicator   _____ Conclusion indicator

10. Seeing that everyone loves ice cream and ice cream is made from milk and milk is very nutritious, it follows that everyone should be encouraged to eat ice cream.

    _____ Premise indicator   _____ Conclusion indicator

5.3 Recognizing Arguments

The Dog in the Rubble Thought Experiment (p. 129):   Here's a passage based on a story from NBCNews.com dated Nov. 29, 2013. Read through this passage and construct an argument related to the story; for example, you could make an argument about the importance of providing emergency shelter for animals as well as people when there is a need to evacuate due to a natural disaster.

Recently a dog named Dexter was found under a pile of rubble nine days after a tornado damaged the apartment building he was living in with his owner, Jacob Montgomery, who is a member of the Illinois National Guard. Dexter was living on the third floor of the appartment building at the time of the tornado. A rescue group going through the rubble looking for animals found him and coaxed him out with hot dogs. He was malnourished, but otherwise he was okay. Dexter was very happy to see Montgomery and showed his happiness by excitedly wagging his tail.

_____

_____

_____

_____

You and classmates will get a chance to evaluate your arguments later, but for now make sure you can identify your conclusion and premise(s).

Conclusion: _____

Premise(s):

_____

_____

_____

Look at the passage about Dexter again. Was it obvious to you when you read it that it wasn't an argument?

_____ Why? _____

_____

An Argument Is Made Up of This (p. 130)

An argument is made up of _____ kinds of statements:

a _____ and _____ .

An Inferential Relationship Means (p. 130)

An inferential relationship means _____

_____

(2 pages)

"To Be Or Not To Be" Practice (pp. 132-133):   Identify which of the problems are arguments and which are not. If you have an argument, then circle the conclusion, but if you have a nonargument, then identify the type of nonargument you have.

1. If it rains, then the baseball game will be postponed.

    _____ Argument _____ Nonargument   Type: _____

2. I believe that the United States should protect the civilians in Syria and stop the carnage.

    _____ Argument _____ Nonargument   Type: _____

3. Cats run faster than dogs. My cat Sammy can out run my dog Maudie. Sammy can also out run the neighbor's dog and does so all the time.

    _____ Argument _____ Nonargument   Type: _____

4. "In December 2011, when Staff Sgt. Jesse Knotts was at his base in Afghanistan mourning the loss of two friends who were killed by a suicide bomber, something unexpected arrived to ease his pain: a cat who suddenly jumped in this lap … He didn't think Koshka (the name he gave the cat) was safe living in Afghanistan, so with the help of a brave local interpreter, Knotts got the animal to Kabul, and his parents footed a $3,000 bill to fly Koshka from there to their home in Oregon."[3]

    _____ Argument _____ Nonargument   Type: _____

5. Sally Ride deserves to receive a national tribute. A national tribute honors someone who had made important contributions to our country. Sally Ride was the first American woman to travel to space and became the third woman in the world to ever travel to space. She was also the first American woman to travel to space a second time. She served on the Augustine committee in 2009 that helped define NASA's spaceflight goals. She inspired other women to join the space program and become astronauts. In addition, she founded Sally Ride Science, a science outreach company that works to encourage students, particularly girls, to study science.

_____ Argument _____ Nonargument   Type: _____

6. Eva Hesse, an American sculptor, is considered one of the most innovative artists of the postwar period. She played a prominent role in the transformation of sculpture in the 1960s by experimenting with a wide range of materials, particularly synthetic materials like latex, plastics, and fiberglass. Her work also challenged Minimalism, the art movement of her time, and helped to create a new genre of art. This challenge is seen, not only in the material she used, but also in the content of her work as she rebelled against the impersonal nature of Minimalism and explored the body and emotion.

_____ Argument _____ Nonargument   Type: _____

7. A state of emergency needs to be declared because of the massive amount of sea lion pups that are starving. Over ten times the usual number of sea lion pups have been rescued and found to be dying due to starvation. There is a tremendous need for an increase in funding to house and rehabilitate the large number of sea lion pups as well as to study the cause and find a solution.

_____ Argument _____ Nonargument   Type: _____

8. If Harry doesn't win the next 800m run, then he will be dropped from the Track team. If he is dropped from the Track team, then he will lose his scholarship. So if Harry doesn't win the next 800m run, he will lose his scholarship.

_____ Argument _____ Nonargument   Type: _____

5.4 Deductive Arguments

 The Beatles Thought Experiment (p. 134): Look at the two arguments about the Beatle Sir Paul McCartney and his song "Yesterday." How are the two arguments different? Does one seem more convincing to you than the other? Why?

The Beatles song "Yesterday" was inspired by a dream, and Sir Paul McCartney wrote the Beatles song "Yesterday." So Sir Paul McCartney wrote a song inspired by a dream.

Sir Paul McCartney claims the tune to his song "Yesterday" was just there one morning in his head when he woke up after dreaming that he had been listening to it being played by a string ensemble, so the song probably came to him in dream.

_____

_____

_____

_____

_____

An Inferential Relationship Is (p. 134)

An inferential relationship is: _____

_____

⭐ **Student Poll** (p. 135): Which of the Beatles arguments has the strongest inferential relationship between the conclusion and the premises?

_____ Argument 1   _____ Argument 2

Do you need to revise your prediction? If so, do it here. (p. 135)

_____

_____

The Clues Quiz (p. 138):   Check the clues that will help you figure out if you have a deductive argument or not. If you get stuck, sneak a peek! When you are done, check your answers. If you have questions or need some help understanding the clues, then get a coach to help you.

_____ Tense of the main verb   _____ Form of the argument

_____ Number of premises   _____ There is a conclusion

_____ Words like certainly or definitely   _____ The truth value of the premises

_____ Actual strength of the relationship between the premises and the conclusion

(2 pages)

Deductive Argument Form Practice (pp. 138-139): For the following problems indicate the deductive argument form, and underline the conclusion.

1. Either Harold gets his driver's license by April 15 or his date will have to drive them to the prom. His date will not have to drive them to the prom. So Harold got his driver's license by April 15.

    _____ Arguments from definition

    _____ Categorical syllogism

    _____ Hypothetical syllogism

    _____ Disjunctive syllogism

    _____ Argument based on mathematics

2. There is a special camaraderie that exists between soldiers who fight together in war. Therefore, there is a special closeness between them.

    _____ Arguments from definition

    _____ Categorical syllogism

    _____ Hypothetical syllogism

    _____ Disjunctive syllogism

    _____ Argument based on mathematics

3. If the University of Oregon beats Oregon State University, then the University of Oregon will
    have bragging rights. The University of Oregon will not have bragging rights. It follows that the
    University of Oregon did not beat Oregon State University.

    _____ Arguments from definition

    _____ Categorical syllogism

    _____ Hypothetical syllogism

    _____ Disjunctive syllogism

    _____ Argument based on mathematics

4. All charged particles have mass. All protons are charged particles. It follows that all protons
    have mass.

    _____ Arguments from definition

    _____ Categorical syllogism

    _____ Hypothetical syllogism

    _____ Disjunctive syllogism

    _____ Argument based on mathematics

5. If a dangerous weather system brings white-out conditions and below zero temperature, then our
    vacation will be cancelled. If our vacation is cancelled, then I will be so bummed out. Therefore, if
    a dangerous weather system brings white-out conditions and below zero temperature, I will be so
    bummed out.

    _____ Arguments from definition

    _____ Categorical syllogism

    _____ Hypothetical syllogism

    _____ Disjunctive syllogism

    _____ Argument based on mathematics

5.5 Inductive Arguments

⭐ **Student Poll** (p. 141):   Think about the inferential claims made in an inductive argument and a deductive argument. If you think the inferential claim is stronger in an inductive argument, then write in the term "inductive argument" on the right side of the tug-of-war, but if you think it is weaker, write it on the left side. Write the term "deductive argument" in the remaining space.

_____   _____

The Apples Argument (p. 141)

Since the eight apples I took from the basket my aunt gave me were delicious, the other six

apples in the basket will probably be delicious too.

What is the conclusion of this argument?

_____

What is the premise?

_____

We have an indicator word clue in this argument about what the premise is. Circle this word in the argument.

Look at the strength of the inferential relationship between the premise and the conclusion. Does the premise guarantee that the other 6 apples in the basket will also be delicious? (p. 142)

_____ Yes   _____ No

Argument From Authority Thought Experiment (p. 144): Read through the two arguments from authority once again, and then answer these questions:

In the first argument who is the authority?

The authority is: _____

Why is this person the authority? _____

_____

If the district attorney has an eyewitness to the murder, why wouldn't we have a guarantee of the truth of the conclusion that Thomas committed the murder? In other words, why do we only have probability regarding the truth that Thomas committed the murder?

_____

_____

_____

In the second argument who is the authority?

The authority is: _____

Why is this person the authority? _____

_____

If our authority is a cardiologist and he says I need a pacemaker, then why is there no guarantee of the truth of the conclusion that I must need one?

_____

_____

_____

Deductive Arguments vs. Inductive Arguments

	Deductive	Inductive
Definition	An argument in which the premises are claimed to provide a guarantee of the truth of the conclusion, so if the premises are true, then it is *impossible* for the conclusion to be false.	An argument in which the premises are claimed to provide only the probability of the truth of the conclusion, so if the premises are true, then it is *improbable or unlikely* that the conclusion is false.
Deductive & Inductive Indicator Words	<ul><li>necessarily</li><li>certainly</li><li>absolutely</li><li>definitely</li></ul>	<ul><li>probably</li><li>improbable</li><li>likely</li><li>unlikely</li><li>reasonable to conclude</li><li>plausible</li><li>implausible</li></ul>
Strength of Inferential Relationship	The conclusion follows with *strict necessity* from the premises.	The conclusion follows only with *probability* from the premises.
Form of Argumentation	<ul><li>arguments from definition</li><li>categorical syllogisms</li><li>hypothetical syllogisms</li><li>disjunctive syllogisms</li><li>arguments based on mathematics</li></ul>	<ul><li>predictive arguments</li><li>arguments from analogy</li><li>inductive generalizations</li><li>arguments from authority</li><li>causal arguments</li></ul>

Deductive vs. Inductive Practice (p. 147): Indicate whether the argument is deductive or inductive, and then identify the form of the argument. Circle the indicator words.

1. The United States women's national soccer team has played four games so far in 2013 and won all of them. So they will probably win the next one too.

   ___ Deductive argument _____   ___ Inductive argument _____

   Form of argument: _____

2. Even though both the side garage door and the back door of the house in the kitchen were found open after the burglary, there were signs that the lock on the back door was pried open, and there was mud on the back doormat and muddy footprints in the kitchen. It is reasonable to conclude that the thief entered through the back door of the kitchen and left through the side garage door.

   ___ Deductive argument _____   ___ Inductive argument _____

   Form of argument: _____

3. If my music teacher said that I do not know my new piece of music, then I need to spend an extra hour every day until the concert practicing it. My music teacher said that I don't know the new piece of music, so it necessarily follows that I need to spend an extra hour every day until the concert practicing it.

   ___ Deductive argument _____   ___ Inductive argument _____

   Form of argument: _____

4. Werewolves are like vampires. In legends both are known to bite humans, move very fast, and run around at night. Vampires also drink blood, therefore, werewolves must drink blood too.

   ___ Deductive argument _____   ___ Inductive argument _____

   Form of argument: _____

(2 pages)

"The Whys" Argument Practice (pp. 148-149): Indicate if the argument is inductive or deductive. Then identify "the Whys" behind you selection, citing the deductive or inductive indicator word, strength of the inferential relationship, and/or form of the argument.

1. Megan is gregarious, so she is very social.

Deductive argument _____   Inductive argument _____

Deductive/inductive indicator words: _____

Inferential relationship: Strict necessity _____   Probability _____

Form of argument: _____

2. I read the first ten books in the Harry Bosh series written by Michael Connelly, so I will probably like the other nine books in the series too.

Deductive argument _____   Inductive argument _____

Deductive/inductive indicator words: _____

Inferential relationship: Strict necessity _____   Probability _____

Form of argument: _____

3. All roses are flowers, and some roses are beautiful. Therefore, some flowers are beautiful.

Deductive argument _____   Inductive argument _____

Deductive/inductive indicator words: _____

Inferential relationship: Strict necessity _____   Probability _____

Form of argument: _____

4. If the Bruno Mars concert begins at 8:00 p.m., then I will be able to eat before the concert. The Bruno Mars concert beings at 8:00 p.m. Therefore, I will be able to eat before the concert.

Deductive argument _____

Inductive argument _____

Deductive/inductive indicator words: _____

Inferential relationship: Strict necessity _____   Probability _____

Form of argument: _____

5. Either Sofia will get the lead in Swan Lake or Isabella will be the one to get the lead. Isabella got the lead in Swan Lake, so Sofia did not get the lead.

Deductive argument _____

Inductive argument _____

Deductive/inductive indicator words: _____

Inferential relationship: Strict necessity _____   Probability _____

Form of argument: _____

6. My iPad was working great before my brother borrowed it, and now my iPad won't turn on. So my brother must have broke it.

Deductive argument _____

Inductive argument _____

Deductive/inductive indicator words: _____

Inferential relationship: Strict necessity _____   Probability _____

Form of argument: _____

5.6 Evaluating Deductive Arguments

(2 pages)

 The "Dogs Really Do Surf!" Thought Experiment (p. 150): Your friend Stacy went to a three-day surfing event in Huntington Beach and then posted on Facebook the following pictures that she found on the Internet after the event.

Later that day you and your friend Rick run into Stacy and the topic of dogs surfing comes up.

Rick: Dogs shouldn't be allowed to go surfing. It isn't safe; they could drown. The owners are forcing their dogs to do something the dogs don't want to do.

Stacy: Dogs should be allowed to go surfing. It is safe; there are people in the water making sure the dogs are safe, many of them wear doggie life jackets, and no dogs have ever drowned. The dogs are having fun. Besides, the competition raises money to help animal welfare organizations. It also brings money that is needed into the community.

Rick: Come on, one of the competition categories is for Best Wipeout—that can't be good for dogs. The owners are putting their dogs at risk.

Stacy: The owners aren't putting their dogs at risk. A wipeout is just part of surfing—even human surfers wipeout. The competition is a lot of fun for everyone. All the dogs get medals, and the winners get surfboard trophies.

Rick: It's also wrong to dress dogs in costumes. This is all about the owners. And even if animal groups and the community get money from this, they are all still using those dogs. I think it is wrong, and it should be stopped.

Which of your friends has the most convincing argument? _____

Here's why:

_____

_____

_____

_____

Which of your friends has the least convincing argument? _____

Here's why:

_____

_____

_____

_____

How did you go about evaluating your two friends' arguments? What criteria did you use?

_____

_____

_____

Testing for a Valid Argument Practice (p. 153): Follow the process for testing for validity, and then decide if each example is valid or not.

Example 1:   All companies that manufacture candy are companies that manufacture food.

Cranberry Sweets is a company that manufactures candy.

Therefore, Cranberry Sweets is a company that manufactures food.

Example 2:   All publishers are companies that manufacture eReaders.

See's Candy is a publisher.

Therefore, See's Candy is a company that manufactures eReaders.

Example 3:   All vegetables are food.

Apples are food.

Therefore, apples are vegetables.

Example 4:   All vegetables are fruit.

Apples are vegetables.

Therefore, apples are fruit.

Example 1:   _____ Yes   _____ No

Example 2:   _____ Yes   _____ No

Example 3:   _____ Yes   _____ No

Example 4:   _____ Yes   _____ No

Testing for a Valid Argument Example 1 Using Diagram (p. 154)

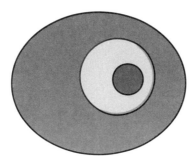

The blue circle represents the group of all companies that manufacture food. The yellow circle represents all the companies that manufacture candy. The red circle represents Cranberry Sweets.

Does Cranberry Sweets (red circle) belong to the circle of companies that manufacture candy (yellow circle)?

_____ Yes   _____ No

Does the circle of companies that manufacture candy (yellow circle) belong to the circle of all the companies that manufacture food (blue circle)?

_____ Yes   _____ No

Testing for a Valid Argument Example 3 Using Diagram (p. 155)

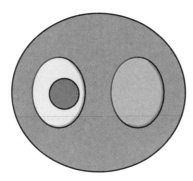

The blue circle represents all food. The yellow circle represents all fruit. The green circle represents all vegetables. The red circle represents all apples.

Is the red circle (apples) in the yellow circle (fruit) or the green circle (vegetables)?

_____ Yellow circle (fruit)   _____ Green circle (vegetables)

Testing for a Sound Argument Examples 1 and 2 (pp. 156-157)

Example 1:   All companies that manufacture candy are companies that manufacture food.

Cranberry Sweets is a company that manufactures candy.

Therefore, Cranberry Sweets is a company that manufactures food.

Do we have a valid argument?   _____ Yes   _____ No

Do we have a sound argument?   _____ Yes   _____ No

Example 2:   All publishers are companies that manufacture eReaders.

See's Candy is a publisher.

Therefore, See's Candy is a company that manufactures eReaders.

Do we have a valid argument?   _____ Yes   _____ No

Do we have a sound argument?   _____ Yes   _____ No

Testing for Soundness Practice I (pp. 157-158): Now it's your turn to test for soundness in our other two examples.

Example 3:   All vegetables are food.

Apples are food.

Therefore, apples are vegetables.

Do we have a valid argument?   _____ Yes   _____ No

Are all the premises true?   _____ Yes   _____ No

Do you have a sound argument?   _____ Yes   _____ No

If you answered no, then identify why.

_____ Invalid argument   _____ At least one premise is not true.

Example 4:   All vegetables are fruit.

Apples are vegetables.

Therefore, apples are fruit.

Do we have a valid argument?   _____ Yes   _____ No

Are all the premises true?   _____ Yes   _____ No

Do you have a sound argument?   _____ Yes   _____ No

If you answered no, then identify why.

_____ Invalid argument   _____ At least one premise is not true

Check-in (p. 158): How's it going? Select your script for this picture, and write it in the dialogue bubble. If none of these work for you, then write your own.

- Looking good! This stuff is easy!

- REALLY! Are you kidding me?!?!

Testing for Soundness Practice II (pp. 160-161)

1. Since *Harry Potter and the Sorcerer's Stone* was written by Shakespeare, and *Harry Potter and the Sorcerer's Stone* is a romance novel, it follows that Shakespeare wrote a romance novel.

   Do we have a valid argument? _____ Yes _____ No

   Are all the premises true? _____ Yes _____ No

   Do you have a sound argument? _____ Yes _____ No

2. Either the pyramids are in Egypt or they are in Rome. The pyramids are in Egypt. Therefore, the pyramids are not in Rome.

   Do we have a valid argument? _____ Yes _____ No

   Are all the premises true? _____ Yes _____ No

   Do you have a sound argument? _____ Yes _____ No

3. If Thomas Jefferson drowned, then Thomas Jefferson died. Thomas Jefferson died. Therefore, Thomas Jefferson drowned.*

   Do we have a valid argument? _____ Yes _____ No

   Are all the premises true? _____ Yes _____ No

   Do you have a sound argument? _____ Yes _____ No

4. No iPhones are made by Samsung. Some smartphones are made by Samsung. So some smartphones are not iPhones.

   Do we have a valid argument? _____ Yes _____ No

   Are all the premises true? _____ Yes _____ No

   Do you have a sound argument? _____ Yes _____ No

*In reality, Thomas Jefferson did not die by drowning.

5. If Lee Harvey Oswald shot President Lincoln, then he is a murderer. Lee Harvey Oswald shot President Lincoln. Therefore, Lee Harvey Oswald is a murderer.

Do we have a valid argument?	_____ Yes	_____ No
Are all the premises true?	_____ Yes	_____ No
Do you have a sound argument?	_____ Yes	_____ No

6. In *Mrs. Doubtfire*, Robin Williams is comical, so he is funny.

Do we have a valid argument?	_____ Yes	_____ No
Are all the premises true?	_____ Yes	_____ No
Do you have a sound argument?	_____ Yes	_____ No

7. Since Queen Elizabeth is Canadian, and Queen Elizabeth is female, we can conclude that at least one ruler of England has been female.

Do we have a valid argument?	_____ Yes	_____ No
Are all the premises true?	_____ Yes	_____ No
Do you have a sound argument?	_____ Yes	_____ No

8. Either *Saturday Night Live* is a comedy or it is a drama. *Saturday Night Live* is not a comedy. Therefore, it is a drama.

Do we have a valid argument?	_____ Yes	_____ No
Are all the premises true?	_____ Yes	_____ No
Do you have a sound argument?	_____ Yes	_____ No

5.7 Evaluating Inductive Arguments

(2 pages)

 The Surfing Goats Thought Experiment (pp. 162-163): You and Rick are talking about the surfing dogs when you meet up with Lakeisha and her boyfriend Tyler. Rick tells Lakeisha about the dogs, and while he's talking she pulls out her phone.[4]

Lakeisha: You think dogs surfing is crazy, then you have to see these pictures of goats surfing at San Onofre State Park in California.

Rick: Ah man, that's so wrong!

Lakeisha: These goats are Pismo the Kid, the billy goat, and Goatee, the nanny goat. They are two of the few surfing goats in the world.

Rick: My aunt has been raising goats for over 20 years. I've been out to her place and seen the goats. They hate it when it rains. My aunt said that they go for shelter faster than the sheep or cows. She said they really hate getting wet. My aunt's an expert on goats, and if she says they hate getting wet, then they do!

Lakeisha: Well, these goats go into the water and have fun surfing, so other goats probably go into the water and have fun surfing too.

Tyler: I have a friend who teaches dogs to surf in San Diego. He says that dogs that surf aren't afraid of the water or they wouldn't get in it, they don't mind surfboards or they wouldn't be on them, and they like to surf. Goats that surf are like these dogs. They aren't afraid of the water or they wouldn't get in it, they also don't mind surfboards or they would't be on them, so they like to surf too.

Which of your friends has the most convincing argument? Why?

Who has the most convincing argument? _____

Here's why:

_____

_____

_____

_____

Who has the least convincing argument? _____

Here's why:

_____

_____

_____

_____

How did you go about evaluating the arguments? What criteria did you use?

_____

_____

_____

The Claims Quiz (p. 164): Every deductive and inductive argument makes two basic claims. Match the name of the claim with what it states. Then identify which claim is tested first by writing them in the order you would test them.

_____ Factual claim   a. That evidence or reasons exist

_____ Inferential claim   b. That the alleged evidence or reasons support something

Test first: _____

Test second: _____

Test the Inferential Claim First (p. 164)

We always test the inferential claim first because:

_____

_____

Stage 1: When We Have a Weak Argument (p. 165)

If we have a weak argument, then we do not need to continue evaluating the argument because:

_____

_____

Testing for a Strong Argument Practice (p. 167): Follow the process for testing for a strong argument, and then decide if each example is strong or weak.

Example 1:   All 5 times I played chess with Carl, I beat him.

I am playing chess with Carl tonight.

Therefore, I will probably beat Carl tonight.

Example 2:   Germany, South Korea, Liberia, St. Lucia, India, Argentina, Iceland, Australia, Brazil, Kosovo, Denmark, Thailand, Jamaica, and Slovenia are places that have traditionally elected men as heads of state but who have eventually elected women as heads of state. The United States is a place that has traditionally elected a man as a head of state. Therefore, in the United States, a woman will probably be elected as head of state eventually too.

Example 3:   Multi-Grammy winner Taylor Swift says Happy Cat cat food is a nutritious food to feed cats. So Happy Cat cat food must be a nutritious food for cats.

Example 4:   Most of the U.S. senators are millionaires. Senator Justin Bieber is a U.S. senator. So Senator Justin Bieber is probably a millionaire.

Example 1:   _____ Strong   _____ Weak

Example 2:   _____ Strong   _____ Weak

Example 3:   _____ Strong   _____ Weak

Example 4:   _____ Strong   _____ Weak

Harder or Easier? (p. 167)

Was testing these inductive arguments to see if they were strong or weak harder or easier than testing the deductive arguments for validity?

_____ Harder _____ Easier   Why? _____

_____

Example 2 – Type of Inductive Argument (p. 167)
In Example 2, what kind of inductive argument do we have?

It is: _____

Example 3 – Type of Inductive Argument (p. 168)
What about example 3? What type of inductive argument is this?

It is: _____

 Check-in (p. 170): Rate your confidence level for understanding how to evaluate inductive arguments. Circle the picture that fits. No clue? Ask a friend or your teacher to coach you.

Easy peasy!

No clue—it's too horrible to say!

Testing for a Cogent Arugment Practice I (p. 171): Now its your turn to evaluate our other three arguments to see if they are cogent or not.

Example 2: Germany, South Korea, Liberia, St. Lucia, India, Argentina, Iceland, Australia, Brazil, Kosovo, Denmark, Thailand, Jamaica, and Slovenia are places that have traditionally elected men as heads of state but who have eventually elected women as heads of state. The United States is a place that has traditionally elected a man as a head of state. Therefore, in the United States, a woman will probably be elected as head of state eventually too. (Note: Premise 1 is true.)

Do you have a strong argument? _____ Yes _____ No

Are all the premises true? _____ Yes _____ No

Any key evidence ignored that requires a different conclusion? _____ Yes _____ No

Do you have a cogent argument? _____ Yes _____ No

Example 3: Seven-time Grammy winner Tayor Swift says Happy Cat cat food is a nutritious food to feed cats. So Happy Cat cat food must be a nutritious food for cats.

Do you have a strong argument? _____ Yes _____ No

Are all the premises true? _____ Yes _____ No

Any key evidence ignored that requires a different conclusion? _____ Yes _____ No

Do you have a cogent argument? _____ Yes _____ No

Example 4: Most of the U.S. senators are millionaires. Senator Justin Bieber is a U.S. senator. So Senator Justin Beiber is probably a millionaire. (Note: Premise 1 is true.)

Do you have a strong argument? _____ Yes _____ No

Are all the premises true? _____ Yes _____ No

Any key evidence ignored that requires a different conclusion? _____ Yes _____ No

Do you have a cogent argument? _____ Yes _____ No

Checking for a Cogent Argument Practice II (pp. 173-174): Evaluate the following inductive arguments.

1. The universe is like a pocket watch. Pocket watches have designers. Therefore, the universe must have a designer.

   Do you have a strong argument? _____ Yes _____ No

   Are all the premises true? _____ Yes _____ No

   Any key evidence ignored that requires a different conclusion? _____ Yes _____ No

   Do you have a cogent argument? _____ Yes _____ No

2. Human models and mannequins are similar. They both have bodies, model clothes, are able to stand very still for long periods of time, and are photographed for advertising. Human models are compensated for their work, so mannequins should be too.

   Do you have a strong argument? _____ Yes _____ No

   Are all the premises true? _____ Yes _____ No

   Any key evidence ignored that requires a different conclusion? _____ Yes _____ No

   Do you have a cogent argument? _____ Yes _____ No

3. Coca-Cola is the most popular soft drink around the world, so somebody, somewhere, is probably drinking Coca-Cola right now. (Note: Premise is true.)

   Do you have a strong argument? _____ Yes _____ No

   Are all the premises true? _____ Yes _____ No

   Any key evidence ignored that requires a different conclusion? _____ Yes _____ No

   Do you have a cogent argument? _____ Yes _____ No

4. Every year the Hawai'i Bowl™ is played in Honolulu, Hawaii, at the Aloha Stadium on Dec. 24 or
    25. The weather year-round is always cold with the majority of the days snowing. Therefore, the
    weather at this year's bowl game at the Aloha Stadium will probably be cold and snowing, too.
    (Premise 1 is true.)

    Do you have a strong argument?   _____ Yes   _____ No

    Are all the premises true?   _____ Yes   _____ No

    Any key evidence ignored that requires a different conclusion?   _____ Yes   _____ No

    Do you have a cogent argument?   _____ Yes   _____ No

5.

    Tyler on the summit of Aconcagua Mountain in
    Argentina on Dec. 27, 2013. He is the youngest
    person (age 9) in recorded history to reach
    this summit.

    Tyler Armstrong, at age 9, reached the summit of
    Aconcagua Mountain, the tallest peak in the Western
    and Southern hemispheres on December 27, 2013. He
    has already reached the summit of Mount Kilimanjaro
    in Tanzania, Africa's tallest peak. Tyler will climb Mount
    McKinley, the highest peak in North America, in 2015.
    Since he has already reached the highest mountains
    on two of the seven continents, one of which is even
    taller than Mount McKinley, he will probably reach the
    summit of Mount McKinley too. (It is true that: (1)
    Aconcagua Mountain is the tallest peak in the Western
    and Southern hemispheres, and (2) Tyler has already
    reached the summit of Mount Kilimanjaro.)

    Do you have a strong argument?   _____ Yes   _____ No

    Are all the premises true?   _____ Yes   _____ No

    Any key evidence ignored that requires a different conclusion?   _____ Yes   _____ No

    Do you have a cogent argument?   _____ Yes   _____ No

Evaluating Deductive and Inductive Arguments

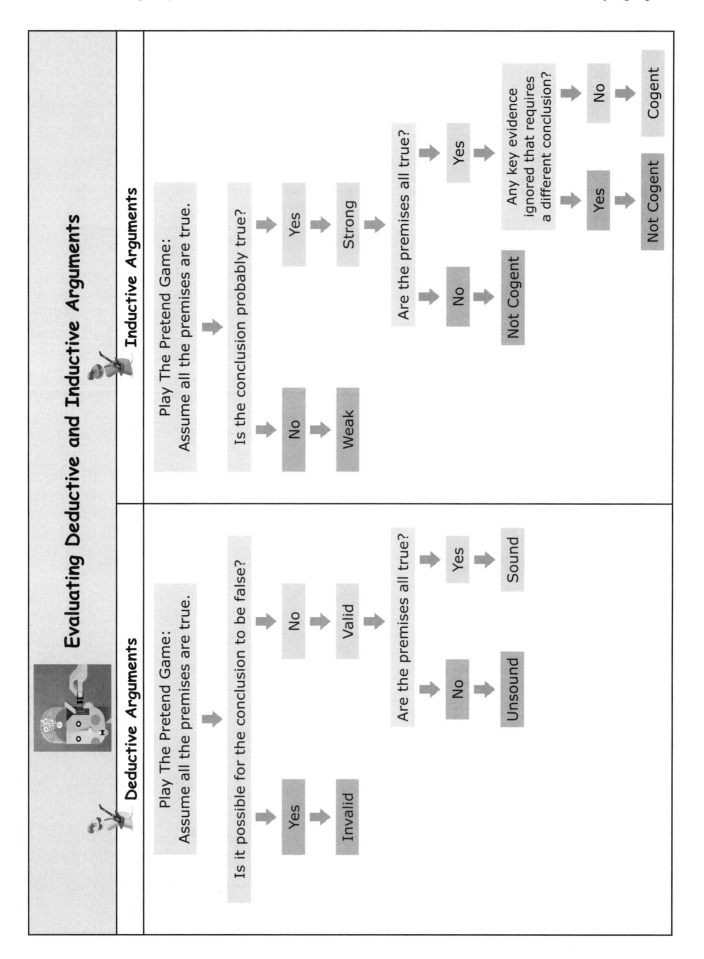

Inductive Arguments

Play The Pretend Game:
Assume all the premises are true.

➔

Is the conclusion probably true?

➔ Yes ➔ Strong ➔ Are the premises all true?

- ➔ Yes ➔ Any key evidence ignored that requires a different conclusion?
  - ➔ No ➔ Cogent
  - ➔ Yes ➔ Not Cogent
- ➔ No ➔ Not Cogent

➔ No ➔ Weak

Deductive Arguments

Play The Pretend Game:
Assume all the premises are true.

➔

Is it possible for the conclusion to be false?

➔ No ➔ Valid ➔ Are the premises all true?

- ➔ Yes ➔ Sound
- ➔ No ➔ Unsound

➔ Yes ➔ Invalid

Important Takeaways

Three important takeaways that I want to remember from this chapter are:

1. _____

   _____

   _____

2. _____

   _____

   _____

3. _____

   _____

   _____

5.9 Individual Activities

Officer on Duty (pp. 179-181)

(3 pages)

You're the Officer on Duty to evaluate arguments, so for the problems on the next two pages, determine if the arguments are deductive or inductive and then evaluate them in the appropriate column. Use the information below to help you as you evaluate the arguments. No key information has been ignored that would require a different conclusion.

- The weatherman said it would be sunny and warm all day today.

- Missy Franklin and Allison Schmitt each won five gold medals in the 2012 Summer Olympics.

- Mark is an introvert.

- Klingons are a humanoid race, and Wookies are large, hairy primate-like creatures who are not humanoid. Frog-dogs are a separate species from Klingons and Wookies.

- Martha Gellhorn, Marie Colvin, Christiane Amanpour, Janine di Giovanni, Kate Adie, Maggie O'Kane, Nima Elbagir, Caryle Murphy, and Charlotte Eager are very famous, accomplished war correspondents.

- Margaret Thatcher was a very famous prime minister of Great Britain.

- Sir Paul McCartney said in an interview about his famous Beatles song "Yesterday," "[It] was entirely magical—I have no idea how I wrote that. I just woke up one morning and it was in my head. I didn't believe it for about two weeks …. [It] was the most complete thing [I'd ever written] …. For something that just happened in a dream, even I have to acknowledge that it was a phenomenal stroke of luck." McCartney says that in his dream he was listening to the tune of the song being played by a classical string ensemble. Sometime later he wrote the words to the song and had it recorded with a string arrangement just has he heard it in his dream.

- I loved the last four pies I bought from Marie Callender; they were fabulous!

1. The weatherman said on the television that it is going to rain today, so it will rain today.

_____ Deductive   _____ Inductive

_____ Valid   _____ Invalid   _____ Strong   _____ Weak

True premises?   _____ Yes _____ No   True premises?   _____ Yes _____ No

Key evidence ignored that requires a different conclusion?   _____ Yes _____ No

_____ Sound   _____ Unsound   _____ Cogent   _____ Not cogent

2. All Olympic gold medalists are amazing athletes. Missy Franklin and Allison Schmitt from the United States each won five gold medals in the 2012 Summer Olympics. It follows that, Missy Franklin and Allison Schmitt are amazing athletes.

_____ Deductive   _____ Inductive

_____ Valid   _____ Invalid   _____ Strong   _____ Weak

True premises?   _____ Yes _____ No   True premises?   _____ Yes _____ No

Key evidence ignored that requires a different conclusion?   _____ Yes _____ No

_____ Sound   _____ Unsound   _____ Cogent   _____ Not cogent

3. Mark is an introvert, so Mark is a person who likes to be the life of every party.

_____ Deductive   _____ Inductive

_____ Valid   _____ Invalid   _____ Strong   _____ Weak

True premises?   _____ Yes _____ No   True premises?   _____ Yes _____ No

Key evidence ignored that requires a different conclusion?   _____ Yes _____ No

_____ Sound   _____ Unsound   _____ Cogent   _____ Not cogent

4. Either Wookies are large hairy primate-like creatures or Wookies are Frog-dogs. Wookies are not Frog-dogs. Therefore, Wookies are large, hairy primate-like creatures.

_____ Deductive   _____ Inductive

_____ Valid   _____ Invalid   _____ Strong   _____ Weak

True premises?   _____ Yes _____ No   True premises?   _____ Yes _____ No

Key evidence ignored that requires a different conclusion?   _____ Yes _____ No

_____ Sound   _____ Unsound   _____ Cogent   _____ Not cogent

5. Margaret Thatcher was the prime minister of Great Britain, so she must be a citizen of Ireland.

_____ Deductive

_____ Valid   _____ Invalid

True premises?   _____ Yes _____ No

_____ Sound   _____ Unsound

_____ Inductive

_____ Strong   _____ Weak

True premises?   _____ Yes _____ No

Key evidence ignored that requires a different conclusion?   _____ Yes _____ No

_____ Cogent   _____ Not cogent

6. Since Martha Gellhorn, Marie Colvine, Christiane Amanpour, Janine di Giovanni, Kate Adie, Maggie O'Kane, Nima Elbagir, Caryle Murphy, and Charlotte Eager are all famous and accomplished war correspondents, and since they are all women, it follows that women can make excellent war correspondents.

_____ Deductive

_____ Valid   _____ Invalid

True premises?   _____ Yes _____ No

_____ Sound   _____ Unsound

_____ Inductive

_____ Strong   _____ Weak

True premises?   _____ Yes _____ No

Key evidence ignored that requires a different conclusion?   _____ Yes _____ No

_____ Cogent   _____ Not cogent

7. Sir Paul McCartney claims the tune to "Yesterday" was just there one morning in his head when he woke up after dreaming of it being played by a string ensemble, so the song probably did come to him in dream.

_____ Deductive

_____ Valid   _____ Invalid

True premises?   _____ Yes _____ No

_____ Sound   _____ Unsound

_____ Inductive

_____ Strong   _____ Weak

True premises?   _____ Yes _____ No

Key evidence ignored that requires a different conclusion?   _____ Yes _____ No

_____ Cogent   _____ Not cogent

8. The last four cherry pies I bought from Marie Callender's restaurant were fabulous, so the next cherry pie I buy will be fabulous too.

_____ Deductive

_____ Valid   _____ Invalid

True premises?   _____ Yes _____ No

_____ Sound   _____ Unsound

_____ Inductive

_____ Strong   _____ Weak

True premises?   _____ Yes _____ No

Key evidence ignored that requires a different conclusion?   _____ Yes _____ No

_____ Cogent   _____ Not cogent

5.10 Group Activities & Discussion

1. **Should Scott Go?** (p. 182)
    In small groups, evaluate Scott's argument from 5.1.

    I should be allowed to go with my friends Kevin and Greg to see Of Monsters and Men, since I'm 17 years old and very responsible. I've never missed my curfew or gotten into trouble and neither has Kevin or Greg. Besides I've kept up my grades all semester.

Here's what you need to know to evaluate the argument: Scott is 17 years old and loves the group Of Monsters and Men. Scott is very responsible; he always gets home when he should, and he has never gotten into trouble. He has two friends named Kevin and Greg. Kevin is also very responsible and has never gotten into trouble. Greg got into trouble last year when he and another friend tagged a building. (Tagging is spray painting your name on something in public, such as a wall.) Since that time he hasn't gotten into trouble. Scott has a B+ average in school this semester.

_____ Deductive			_____ Inductive		
_____ Valid	_____ Invalid		_____ Strong	_____ Weak	
True premises?	_____ Yes _____ No		True premises?	_____ Yes _____ No	
			Key evidence ignored that requires a different conclusion?	_____ Yes _____ No	
_____ Sound	_____ Unsound		_____ Cogent	_____ Not cogent	

Once the small groups have their answers, then discuss this argument as a large group. If the argument is either not sound or not cogent, then discuss how Scott could have made a sound or cogent argument. In the end, are they convinced by Scott's argument? Should Scott be allowed to go to the concert? Why or why not?

2. **Our Evaluation** (pp. 182-183)   (2 pages)

   In small groups of four, students will evaluate one another's arguments from *Your Argument Thought Experiment* in section 5.2. Have students make copies of their arguments for the other students in their groups. (Use the worksheet on page R119.) Once this is done, have them identify one argument from their group that the class as a large group will evaluate. As a large group evaluate each of the arguments together. Discuss how the arguments could be made sound or cogent if they are not.

                                                                              (2 pages)

3. **Dog in the Rubble** (p. 184)

   In small groups evaluate each other's argument from *The Dog in the Rubble Thought Experiment* in section 5.3. Have students make copies of thier arguments for those in their group. (Use the same worksheet on page R118.) If any of the arguments are not sound or cogent, then have the students in the small groups help one another think of ways to make them sound or cogent. Finally, have the groups identify an argument to work with in the large group. This may be an argument that needs some help to be made sound or cogent.

Evaluation Worksheet for Use with Activity 2 (p. 182) and Activity 3 (p. 184)

Name: _____

_____ Deductive   _____ Inductive

_____ Valid   _____ Invalid   _____ Strong   _____ Weak

True premises?   _____ Yes _____ No   True premises?   _____ Yes _____ No

                                                    Key evidence ignored that requires a different
                                                    conclusion?   _____ Yes _____ No

_____ Sound   _____ Unsound   _____ Cogent   _____ Not cogent

Name: _____

_____ Deductive   _____ Inductive

_____ Valid   _____ Invalid   _____ Strong   _____ Weak

True premises?   _____ Yes _____ No   True premises?   _____ Yes _____ No

                                                    Key evidence ignored that requires a different
                                                    conclusion?   _____ Yes _____ No

_____ Sound   _____ Unsound   _____ Cogent   _____ Not cogent

Name: _____

_____ Deductive   _____ Inductive

_____ Valid   _____ Invalid   _____ Strong   _____ Weak

True premises?   _____ Yes _____ No   True premises?   _____ Yes _____ No

                                                    Key evidence ignored that requires a different
                                                    conclusion?   _____ Yes _____ No

_____ Sound   _____ Unsound   _____ Cogent   _____ Not cogent

Name: _____

_____ Deductive   _____ Inductive

_____ Valid   _____ Invalid   _____ Strong   _____ Weak

True premises?   _____ Yes _____ No   True premises?   _____ Yes _____ No

                                                    Key evidence ignored that requires a different
                                                    conclusion?   _____ Yes _____ No

_____ Sound   _____ Unsound   _____ Cogent   _____ Not cogent

4. **Surfing Dogs** (p. 184)

In small groups have the students discuss their answers to *The 'Dogs Really do Surf!' Thought Experiment* in section 5.6. Then students are to analyze the parts of the arguments Rick and Stacy make. While Rick and Stacy make arguments and counter arguments, students are to identify the main conclusion and the main premises or reasons that support that conclusion. Once the small groups come to a consensus about the two arguments, discuss them as a large group. Also have the large group discuss which of the two arguments is the most convincing and why.

<u>Rick's argument</u>

Conclusion: _____

Premise 1: _____

Premise 2: _____

Premise 3: _____

Premise 4: _____

Premise 5: _____

<u>Stacy's argument</u>

Conclusion: _____

Premise 1: _____

Premise 2: _____

Premise 3: _____

Premise 4: _____

Premise 5: _____

Premise 6: _____

5. **Surfing Goats** (p. 185)
In small groups have the students identify the type of inductive arguments each arguer makes
in **The Surfing Goats Thought Experiment** in section 5.7 and their reasons why they selected
the type they did. Also have them identify the conclusion of the arguments. Finally, they are to
discuss which argument they think is the most convincing and why. Follow up with a large group
discussion.

<u>Rick's argument</u>

Type of argument: _____

Reasons: _____

_____

_____

Conclusion: _____

<u>Lakeisha's argument</u>

Type of argument: _____

Reasons: _____

_____

_____

Conclusion: _____

<u>Tyler's argument</u>

Type of argument: _____

Reasons: _____

_____

_____

Conclusion: _____

6.1 What are Fallacies?

⭐ **Student Poll** (p. 186): On a scale from 1 ("Really awful!") to 10 ("Totally awesome!"), rate the reasoning in the following argument.

> One student to another student:
>
> "I didn't get the lead in the musical because my sign is Aries,
>
> a fire sign, and Mrs. Lawson, who's directing, is a water sign—
>
> Cancer. Everyone knows these are the least compatible signs."

I give the reasoning in this argument a _____.

💡 **The "Why Should I Care?" Thought Experiment** (p. 187): You're a critical thinker, so why should you care about fallacies? Crank out your best thinking around this and come up with an example that shows why caring matters (in other words, think of an example of what might happen if we didn't care).

It is important to care about fallacies because:

_____

_____

_____

_____

Here's my example that shows why caring about fallacies matters:

_____

_____

_____

_____

6.2 Fallacies of Relevance

My Prediction (p. 188)

"Dude, people who wear green or take anything green into the ocean, especially a green board, drown. So, if you take that green board in, you'll drown."

I think you'll be telling me about _____

_____

Appeal to Force

⭐ **Student Poll** (p. 190): Does the following argument commit the fallacy appeal to force? Choose "Yes" or "No."

President Obama to the government of Syria, via a news conference at the White House, on the use of chemical weapons or their being moved because of the threat posed to the people of Syria, U.S. allies, and to the United States:

"We cannot have a situation in which chemical or biological weapons are falling into the hands of the wrong people. We have been clear to the Assad regime, but also to other players on the ground, that a red line for us is we start seeing a whole bunch of weapons moving around or being utilized. That would change my calculus [about American military intervention]. That would change my equation."

_____ Yes, this argument commits the fallacy of appeal to force.

_____ No, this argument does not commit the fallacy of appeal to force.

Appeal to Pity

💡 **Argument from Compassion Thought Experiment** (p. 193): Think of a person, a group of people, animals etc. that need help. Create your own argument from compassion. Remember to provide genuine reasons why they deserve special consideration and how this special consideration will help.

_____

_____

_____

_____

Ad Hominem

⭐ **Student Poll** (p. 194): On a scale from 1 ("Not at all!") to 10 ("I'm sold!"), rate how persuasive each of the arguments are in the examples.

Example 1:   Web teacher explaining *ad hominem* abusive (tongue-in-cheek):

"*Ad hominem* is a logical fallacy in which you attack your opponent rather than attacking your opponent's argument. It's an appropriate name, too, since it sounds like a Neanderthal species, and that's about what you're dealing with in the types of people who make those types of arguments … Aw, man …."[2]

Example 2:   Critic of U2's rock star front man Bono who campaigns against world debt for the world's poorest countries and calls for the cancellation of Third World debt: "Why should the world's leaders listen to Bono talk about world debt when he's nothing but a neoliberal puppet and an ambassador for imperial exploitation?"

_____ Example 1   _____ Example 2

💡 **The Considering Someone's Circumstances Thought Experiment** (p. 196): Is it ever appropriate to consider someone's circumstance?

_____ Yes, always   _____ Yes, sometimes   _____ No, never

Explain your answer.

_____

_____

_____

_____

2. Chad Jones, "Logical Fallacies: Ad hominem," *The Collapsed Wave Function*, Science blog, Jan. 9, 2012, http://www.thecollapsedwavefunction.com.

(2 pages)

 Fallacies of Relevance Practice (pp. 198-199): In the following problems indicate whether or not a fallacy is being committed. If one is, then identify which one. Finally explain your reason for selecting that particular fallacy.

1. Sallie should be promoted to the position as supervisor because she is a single mom with three children to take care of. One of the boys needs new glasses and the other one needs braces. The oldest one needs money for college this year.

_____ No fallacy committed   _____ Fallacy committed

_____ Appeal to force   _____ Appeal to pity

_____ Ad hominem

My reason: _____

_____

2. The interest rate on student loans should not be increased. Students are forced to borrow huge amounts to fund their ever increasing educational costs, and by increasing the interest rate, students will have an economic burden that will be difficult to pay back, will impact their future standard of living, cause more loan defaults, and will discourage young people from getting a college education.

_____ No fallacy committed   _____ Fallacy committed

_____ Appeal to force   _____ Appeal to pity

_____ Ad hominem

My reason: _____

_____

3. Of course, Warren Buffet argues for increasing the tax rates for high-income taxpayers. He doesn't care about giving money away. He gave half of his billion dollar fortune to charity already, which shows that dementia must have set in, and his crazy ramblings on these tax increases proves that.

_____ No fallacy committed   _____ Fallacy committed

_____ Appeal to force   _____ Appeal to pity

_____ Ad hominem

My reason: _____

_____

4. If wealthy individuals are hiring disabled people to pose as family members so that their family can cut to the front of the line for rides at Disneyland, then what they are doing violates the intention of Disneyland's policy regarding disabled guests. If what they are doing violates the intention of Disneyland's policy regarding disabled guests, then they and the disabled person participating in this should be banned from all Disneyland amusement parks. Therefore, if wealthy individuals are hiring disabled people to pose as family members so that their family can cut to the front of the line for rides, then they and the disabled person participating in this should be banned from all Disneyland amusement parks.

    _____ No fallacy committed   _____ Fallacy committed

    _____ Appeal to force   _____ Appeal to pity

                         _____ Ad hominem

    My reason: _____

    _____

5. I know that some of the part-time instructors at the college are in favor of forming a union, and we all know that would not benefit the school. Next month I am scheduled to review contracts and decide who will receive a contract for the next term. I sure would hate to lose anyone.

    _____ No fallacy committed   _____ Fallacy committed

    _____ Appeal to force   _____ Appeal to pity

                         _____ Ad hominem

    My reason: _____

    _____

6.3 Fallacies of Presumption

⭐ **Student Poll** (p. 200): On a scale from 1 ("So bad!") to 10 ("Best ever!"), rate the quality of the evidence provided in the argument below.

> The best surfer is the one who has the ability to read and catch waves because a surfer
>
> who rips out in the water knows where to be and can continually get in the right spot.

I rate the quality of the evidence as a _____.

I chose this rating because: _____

_____

Begging the Question

Missing Premise (p. 201)

> Murder is morally wrong; therefore, active euthanasia is morally wrong.[3]

If you aren't sure what active euthanasia is, then see footnote 4 below.[4] What premise is missing in this argument? Can you tell? Look at the argument again, and write what you think the missing premise is.

Missing premise: _____

Here's a clue for you regarding the missing premise. How did we get from murder to active euthanasia—what's the connection? Now try once again to provide the missing premise.

Missing premise: _____

3. This example is taken from "Fallacies," University of North Carolina Writing Center, http://writingcenter.unc.edu/handouts/fallacies/.

4. Active euthanasia is a means of ending life through the use of medication by a medical doctor. The primary intent is to end the patient's life at the patient's request, and the context for allowing it is terminal illness, immense suffering, and a prolonged death. It is often called "mercy killing." Basically, this is what occurs when an animal that is suffering is euthanized by a veterinarian (though sometimes other factors may also be involved).

False Dichotomy

⭐ **Student Poll** (p. 203): Rate the following statements about Examples 1 and 2.

1 = "For sure!"   2 = "No way!"

Example 1:   Malia to her parents:

"Either you let me go to the Black Keys concert with Philip or you'll run my love

life. I know you don't want to ruin my love life, so I'm sure you'll let me go to

the concert with Philip."

Example 2:   Judy to her boyfriend Sam:

"Either you become a vegetarian or you don't care about animals.

You won't become a vegetarian, so you obviously don't care about animals."

_____ 1. If Malia does not go to the concert, then her love life will be ruined.

_____ 2. Malia provides her parents with the only two possible alternatives.

_____ 3. Judy is right that either you're a vegetarian or you don't care about animals.

_____ 4. Only one of these examples commits a fallacy.

John's Disjunctive Argument (pp. 204-205)

John to parents:

"Either you will buy me a new car to drive to school or I will have to drive this old death trap

that is dangerous and could get me killed."

Given the disjunctive premise, what do you think the conclusion is?

The conclusion is: _____

What is the missing premise?

The missing premise is: _____

_____

Driving the Old Death Trap Thought Experiment (p. 205): Help John out by providing some other alternatives besides the two he has in his argument. Come up with at least two of them.

_____

_____

_____

_____

Do you need to revise your prediction? If so, do it here. (p. 205)

_____

_____

(2 pages)

 Fallacies of Presumption Practice (pp. 207-208): In the following problems indicate whether or not a fallacy is being committed. If one is, then identify which one. Finally, explain your reason for selecting that particular fallacy.

1. Wood sawdust is combustible, therefore it burns.

    _____ No fallacy committed   _____ Fallacy committed

    _____ Begging the question   _____ False dichotomy

                            _____ Suppressed evidence

    My reason: _____

    _____

2. Either our next truck will be a Ford F-150 4WD or we will go bankrupt paying for gasoline. We don't want to go bankrupt paying for gasoline, so our next truck will be a Ford F-150 4WD.

    _____ No fallacy committed   _____ Fallacy committed

    _____ Begging the question   _____ False dichotomy

                            _____ Suppressed evidence

    My reason: _____

    _____

3. Either you take a smaller suitcase on the trip or you will never go on another vacation.

    _____ No fallacy committed   _____ Fallacy committed

    _____ Begging the question   _____ False dichotomy

                            _____ Suppressed evidence

    My reason: _____

    _____

4. Bigfoot must exist because people have seen Bigfoot. People have taken photos of a large hairy apelike creature in the woods. This would not be possible if people hadn't seen Bigfoot, and surely people could never see Bigfoot if Bigfoot didn't exist.

_____ No fallacy committed   _____ Fallacy committed

_____ Begging the question   _____ False dichotomy

_____ Suppressed evidence

My reason: _____

_____

5. Martina Navratilova is the greatest female tennis player of all time. She achieved the longest winning streak in women's or men's tennis history; three of the longest winning streaks by any female tennis player; and a Grand Slam, playing in 85 Grand Slam finals in singles and doubles. She also won 9 Wimbledon titles and played in 12 Wimbledon finals, won the U.S. Open 4 times, won the Australian Open 3 times, and won the French Open 2 times.

_____ No fallacy committed   _____ Fallacy committed

_____ Begging the question   _____ False dichotomy

_____ Suppressed evidence

My reason: _____

_____

6. If Judith wins her next singles match at the team tryouts, then she will be on the tennis team. Judith won her next singles match at the team tryouts, so she will be on the tennis team.

_____ No fallacy committed   _____ Fallacy committed

_____ Begging the question   _____ False dichotomy

_____ Suppressed evidence

My reason: _____

_____

6.4 Fallacies of Weak Induction

Appeal to Unqualified Authority

⭐ **Student Poll** (p. 210): On a scale from 1 ("Not trustworthy!") to 10 ("Very trustworthy!"), rate the quality of the authorities.

Example 1:   Ms. Truthwell, the district attorney, argued that there was irrefutable evidence that Sam Thomas murdered the chef at La Masion because Mr. O'Toole, the 80-year-old man who was eating in the restaurant, testified that he saw Thomas shoot the chef.

Example 2:   "Dr. Hart, a cardiologist, said that I need a pacemaker, so I must need one."

_____ Mr. O'Toole, eyewitness to the murder of the chef

_____ Dr. Hart, cardiologist

Explain why you rated each person the way you did.

Mr. O'Toole: _____

_____

Dr. Hart: _____

_____

False Cause

💡 **The Surfboard Thought Experiment** (p. 211): Imagine that you are the guy in the photo with the surfboard on the way to the beach when some guy says this to you:

"Dude, people who wear green or take anything green into the ocean, especially a green board, drown. So, if you take that green board in, you'll drown."

Do you buy his argument? Why or why not?

_____

_____

_____

What would you say to him in response?

_____

_____

_____

⭐ **Student Poll** (p. 213): On a scale from 1 ("Utter nonsense! Wash your socks!") to 10 ("Makes perfect sense to me!") rate the son's argument: _____

Example 1:   Son to his mom:

"You can't wash my game socks. I've worn them for the last three weeks, and

I've made every basket I've attempted."

Have you ever heard an athlete saky something like that before? _____ Yes _____ No

Have you ever thought or said something like that before?   _____ Yes _____ No

Why do you think people think like the son? Do you think it affects their results?

_____

_____

_____

⭐ **Student Poll** (p. 214): Check all the factors that you think have impacted why children read below grade level.

_____ Time spent playing video games   _____ Time spent watching TV

_____ "Dumbed-down" educational resources   _____ Time spent playing sports

_____ Poor teaching of reading in schools   _____ Poverty

_____ Not enough emphasis on reading comprehension and vocabulary

_____ Not enough books for all the children in a class to use

_____ Role of parents in encouraging their children to read

Other: _____

(2 pages)

 Fallacies of Weak Induction Practice (pp. 217-218): In the following problems indicate whether or not a fallacy is being committed. If one is, then identify which one. Finally, explain your reason for selecting that particular fallacy.

1. Beyoncé says that the Kia Optima is the safest car on the market and that it is the best car to buy, so it must be the best car to buy.

   _____ No fallacy committed   _____ Fallacy committed

   _____ Appeal to unqualified authority   _____ False cause

   _____ Hasty generalization

   My reason: _____

   _____

2. Every time I watch television, my mom has chores for me to do. If I quit watching television, then I won't have to do chores anymore.

   _____ No fallacy committed   _____ Fallacy committed

   _____ Appeal to unqualified authority   _____ False cause

   _____ Hasty generalization

   My reason: _____

   _____

3. CNN is terrible at reporting news. During CNN's coverage of the Boston Marathon bombings, CNN wrongly reported early on that a suspect had been arrested when that wasn't true. In fact, the FBI had to issue a statement correcting CNN's mistake.

   _____ No fallacy committed   _____ Fallacy committed

   _____ Appeal to unqualified authority   _____ False cause

   _____ Hasty generalization

   My reason: _____

   _____

4. I played Nintendo Wii last Saturday over at John's house. The motion gaming was fun, but the graphics just aren't there like they are with my Xbox 360, and Nintendo Wii doesn't have a processor that will play the kind of games I play on my Xbox. The Xbox 360 has the best online community too. The Xbox 360 is better.

    _____ No fallacy committed   _____ Fallacy committed

    _____ Appeal to unqualified authority   _____ False cause

    _____ Hasty generalization

    My reason: _____

    _____

5. This first day of American Literature class dragged on forever. I can tell it is going to be a boring course.

    _____ No fallacy committed   _____ Fallacy committed

    _____ Appeal to unqualified authority   _____ False cause

    _____ Hasty generalization

    My reason: _____

    _____

6. The increase in vandalism, particularly graffiti, in U.S. National Parks is due to the use of social media that allows the vandals to get instant gratification and recognition for what they've done.

    _____ No fallacy committed   _____ Fallacy committed

    _____ Appeal to unqualified authority   _____ False cause

    _____ Hasty generalization

    My reason: _____

    _____

6.5 Fallacies of Ambiguity

⭐ **Student Poll** (p. 219): See if you can figure out if any of these arguments commit the fallacy of equivocation. Then rate them with either a 1 ("No way!"), 2 ("Absolutely!")

_____ 1. Only man is rational. No woman is a man. Therefore, no woman is rational.

_____ 2. "Kevin told me he pitches a wicked fastball, so his fastball pitches must be dangerous."

_____ 3. A Chihuahua is a dog, so a large Chihuahua is a large dog.

_____ 4. The press had a duty to publish all the details of Marilyn Monroe's private life because of the public interest in her mysterious death. Besides, the press always has a responsibility to print stories that are in the public interest.

Was it easy to figure out if these arguments committed the fallacy of equivocation? Some were probably easy and may even have seemed silly, but they get the point across. Now, for those that you gave a "2," identify the number of the argument and what has been equivocated in the argument.

Argument number and what has been equivocated: _____

_____

_____

_____

Amphiboly

(3 pages)

💡 **Amphiboly Thought Experiment** (pp. 221-223): Read through each example and try to identify what is causing the ambiguity, and then explain the two different ways you could understand it.

Example 1[5]:

LIONS
STAY IN YOUR CAR

"We'd better not get out here."

The problem is due to: _____

_____

The two ways of interpreting this are:

1. _____

2. _____

5. This cartoon is based on an idea of another cartoon whose content is found in "Fallacies" in the Internet Encyclopedia of Philosophy, http://www.iep.utm.edu.

Example 2:

Wife to husband: "Look at this headline, Henry. The Juvenile Court is going to start shooting kids. This is not the way to stop juvenile crime. They cannot be allowed to do this."

The problem is due to: _____

_____

The two ways of interpreting this are:

1. _____

2. _____

Example 3:

June Sullivan, Barbara Sikes' lawyer, to the jury:

"The contract signed by both parties reads, 'In exchange for building a treehouse in my yard to be used as a writer's retreat, I, Barbara Sikes, promise to pay my nephew Fred Sally $25,000 and give him my pool table only if he finishes the job by July 1, 2014.' Therefore, since Fred Sally did not finish building the treehouse until August 17, it follows that he gets neither the $25,000 nor the pool table."

The problem is due to: _____

_____

Fred Sally and Barbara Sikes have two different ways of interpreting the contract.

Fred Sally interprets the contract this way:

_____

_____

Barbara Sikes interprets the contract this way:

_____

_____

Fallacies of Ambiguity Practice (pp. 225-226): In the following problems indicate whether or not a fallacy is being committed. If one is, then identify which one. Finally, explain your reason for selecting that particular fallacy.

1. The police would not disclose the name of the woman who drove her car off the side of the mountain at the request of her husband. So her husband must not care what happens to her.

   _____ No fallacy committed   _____ Fallacy committed

   _____ Equivocation   _____ Amphiboly

   My reason: _____

   _____

2. Berthe Morisot is one of the greatest Impressionist painters. She and her work were admired by the other Impressionist painters, many of whom bought her paintings. She was also very popular with the public, outselling even Monet and Renoir.

   _____ No fallacy committed   _____ Fallacy committed

   _____ Equivocation   _____ Amphiboly

   My reason: _____

   _____

3. Giving money to the Red Cross is the right thing to do. So the Red Cross has a right to our money.

   _____ No fallacy committed   _____ Fallacy committed

   _____ Equivocation   _____ Amphiboly

   My reason: _____

   _____

4. If we buy an airline ticket now we can save 40% and that means 40% more vacation for us.

_____ No fallacy committed   _____ Fallacy committed

_____ Equivocation   _____ Amphiboly

My reason: _____

_____

5. We should travel by plane on our trip to Missouri since traveling such a long distance by car is exhausting and boring.

_____ No fallacy committed   _____ Fallacy committed

_____ Equivocation   _____ Amphiboly

My reason: _____

_____

6. Madge said that despite being declared mentally incompetent, Shelia Sherry's lawyer tried to see to it that her claim to her inheritance was protected. I don't think it is right that the court let Shelia be represented by a lawyer who's been declared mentally incompetent.

_____ No fallacy committed   _____ Fallacy committed

_____ Equivocation   _____ Amphiboly

My reason: _____

_____

6.6 Detecting and Avoiding Fallacies

 Check-in (p. 227): Rate your confidence level for understanding fallacies. Circle the picture that fits. No clue? Ask a friend or your teacher to coach you.

Got it & grooving!

No clue!

The "Why Commit Fallacies?" Thought Experiment (p. 227): Think about why people might commit fallacies and then create characters to exemplify the reasons. You need two. Hint: If one of the reasons is that some people commit fallacies because of poor critical thinking skills, then create a profile of that kind of person. Give the person a name, background, etc. Have some fun with it.

Reason 1: _____

_____

Character 1: _____

_____

Reason 2: _____

_____

Character 2: _____

_____

⭐ **Student Poll** (p. 228): Which of the fallacies we studied might be persuasive and trick you? Check all that apply.

_____ Appeal to force

_____ Ad hominem

_____ False dichotomy

_____ Appeal to unqualified authority

_____ Hasty generalization

_____ Amphiboly

_____ Appeal to pity

_____ Begging the question

_____ Suppressed evidence

_____ False Cause

_____ Equivocation

_____ None

The Fallacies Quiz (pp. 229-230): Circle the best answer for each problem.

1. The fallacy of _____ involves some type of psychological or physical harm.

    a. Appeal to pity   b. Appeal to force   c. *Ad hominem* abusive

2. In the fallacy of appeal to force the threat of harm is substituted for:

    a. Compassion   b. A false dichotomy   c. Genuine evidence.

3. Oversimplified cause is a type of fallacy called _____.

    a. Hasty generalization   b. False cause   c. Equivocation

4. In the fallacy of _____ the problem of ambiguity occurs due to the meaning of words.

    a. Equivocation   b. Amphiboly   c. Begging the question

5. The focus of the _____ fallacies is to attack someone's character or circumstances instead of providing genuine evidence.

    a. *Ad hominem*   b. False cause   c. Suppressed evidence

6. In the fallacy of _____ the causal connection between cause and effect is at best highly questionable and at worst does not exist at all.

    a. Suppressed evidence   b. False cause   c. False dichotomy

7. In the fallacy of _____ the argument may leave out a key premise, restate the conclusion as a premise, or use circular reasoning.

    a. Hasty generalization   b. False cause   c. Begging the question

8. The clue to recognizing the fallacy of _____ is to realize that there really are more options than the two being presented.

    a. Suppressed evidence   b. Equivocation   c. False dichotomy

9. The key to telling the difference between a valid argument that evokes sympathetic feelings/compassion and the fallacy of _____ is to be able to tell the difference between genuine evidence and emotional appeal.

    a. Appeal to unqualified authority   b. Appeal to pity   c. Begging the question

10. The clue for identifying the fallacy of _____ is to see if the conclusion is based on a sample that is representative of the group from which it is taken or one that is too small or atypical.

    a. Hasty generalization   b. Suppressed evidence   c. False cause

The Fallacies Quiz Answers (p. 232): Check your answers and then add up your points (1 point for each right answer). Discover the level of training you are at.

Answers: 1. b
   2. c
   3. b
   4. a
   5. a

   6. b
   7. c
   8. c
   9. b
   10. a

Fallacy Master: 10

You have mastered the material. You know how to recognize fallacies and not be taken in by them. You are ready to coach others on fallacies.

Fallacy Knight: 8-9

You have shown you are competent in recognizing and understanding fallacies. Keep practicing so that you can become a Fallacy Master.

Fallacy Apprentice: 6-7

You still are learning and need more study and practice before you have mastered the competency you need. Keep working on them and soon you will be able to spot them and protect yourself from being taken in by them or using them yourself.

Fallacy Initiate: 5 & under

You have demonstrated that you understand the basics but that you need more work and practice before you can master fallacies. Seek a coach and don't get discouraged. You can do it!

My score is: _____

My level of training is: _____

If your level of training isn't where you want it to be, then consider getting someone to coach you on informal fallacies.

 Here are some specific tips Gladys has for you about the fallacies in this chapter that will help you detect when they're occurring (pp. 233-234):

Fallacy	Tips
Appeal to Force	Is the threat of physical or psychological harm substituted for genuine evidence? Is the threat of force relevant to the conclusion? Does the evidence support the conclusion?
Appeal to Pity	Have pathetic circumstances been substituted for genuine evidence? Is the arguer trying to hook your emotions in order to get you to accept the argument? Does the evidence support the conclusion?
Ad Hominem	Is the argument focused only on attacking the person's character or circumstances instead of providing genuine evidence as to why the opponent's argument is wrong? Is there verbal abuse or name-calling in order to discredit the argument? Is the arguer simply attacking a perceived motive and failing to provide real evidence? Does the evidence support the conclusion?
Begging the Question	Does the evidence actually support the conclusion or is it merely an illusion that it does? Has a key premise been left out, one that is controversial or difficult to establish the truth of, but necessary for the soundness of the argument? Do the premises merely restate the conclusion? Does the argument have circular reasoning?
False Dichotomy	Are there really only two options and no other alternatives exist?

 Gladys isn't done serving up tips for you!

Fallacy	Tips
Suppressed Evidence	Has relevant evidence been left out that if known would lead to a different conclusion?
Appeal to Unqualified Authority	Is the authority trustworthy or reliable? Is the authority an expert on the subject & relevant to the argument? Is the authority biased, have a motive to lie, have some physical or medical problems that affect either perception or memory? Does the testimony provide genuine evidence for the conclusion?
False Cause	Is this only a correlation or is there really a causal connection between the two events? Could there be other factors that are also responsible for the cause besides the one the arguer identified?
Hasty Generalization	Is the conclusion based on a sample that is too small or atypical? Is the conclusion based on a stereotype?
Equivocation	Is there more than one meaning for the key words or phrases used in the argument, and does the meaning of these words or phrases shift in any way?
Amphiboly	Is there ambiguity in the argument? Is the ambiguity because one of the premises can be interpreted in two different ways due to an error in grammar or punctuation? And is the conclusion based on the wrong interpretation of that ambiguity?

Important Takeaways

Three important takeaways that I want to remember from this chapter are:

1. _____

   _____

   _____

2. _____

   _____

   _____

3. _____

   _____

   _____

6.8 Individual Activities

The Fallacy Inspection (pp. 238-241): For the following problems: (4 pages)

- Indicate whether or not a fallacy is being committed.

- If a fallacy is being committed, then identify the fallacy.

- Explain your reason for selecting a particular fallacy.

1. One morning I shot an elephant in my pajamas. How he got in my pajamas I'll never know.

— Groucho Marx in *Animal Crackers*

_____ No fallacy   _____ Fallacy

Name of fallacy: _____

Reason: _____

_____

2. Every bestselling novel I've ever written was written at my retreat in Vermont. So if I cannot write my next novel there, it will be a flop.

_____ No fallacy   _____ Fallacy

Name of fallacy: _____

Reason: _____

_____

3. After coming out of a coma, the detective asked the victim who attacked her. That detective is sure dedicated to go to work right after coming out of a coma.

_____ No fallacy   _____ Fallacy

Name of fallacy: _____

Reason: _____

_____

4. John, it would be a good idea if the organization cut its budget by $25,000. I know you are well aware that in the past the board has had no problem firing a CEO who didn't do what he was told to do.

_____ No fallacy   _____ Fallacy

Name of fallacy: _____

Reason: _____

_____

5. Useless courses like English literature should not be taught in high school because they are a waste because they are worthless.

_____ No fallacy   _____ Fallacy

Name of fallacy: _____

Reason: _____

_____

6. Yesterday I watched the film *A.I. Artificial Intelligence* written by Steven Spielberg and it was terrible. He needs to stick with directing and quit trying to write screenplays.

_____ No fallacy   _____ Fallacy

Name of fallacy: _____

Reason: _____

_____

7. Leslie tries to convince the public about the value of building a park:
"Wouldn't you rather have a park than a storage facility for nuclear waste?"
— Leslie Knope in *Parks and Recreation*

_____ No fallacy   _____ Fallacy

Name of fallacy: _____

Reason: _____

_____

8. When it comes to lung transplants, the sickest person should receive the first available donation regardless of the person's age. The organ allocation policies state that organ allocation is supposed to be based on who is the sickest and not an arbitrary age of 12 as it is in the lung allocation guidelines.

_____ No fallacy   _____ Fallacy

Name of fallacy: _____

Reason: _____

_____

9. You should give me all the points for the essay on the exam. I really tried hard, and I wrote a lot on the exam despite feeling sick and having to stay up late babysitting my little brother while my parents were visiting my grandmother who fell and broke her hip.

_____ No fallacy   _____ Fallacy

Name of fallacy: _____

Reason: _____

_____

10. The quality of education in our high schools has been getting worse for years. This is due to the fact that the reading level in the textbooks gets lower every year.

_____ No fallacy   _____ Fallacy

Name of fallacy: _____

Reason: _____

_____

11. "But I don't want to go among mad people," Alice remarked.

"Oh, you can't help that," said the Cat, "we're all mad here. I'm mad. Your mad."

"How do you know I'm mad?" said Alice.

"You must be, "said the Cat, "or you wouldn't have come here."

—*Alice In Wonderland* by Lewis Carroll

_____ No fallacy   _____ Fallacy

Name of fallacy: _____

Reason: _____

_____

12. Candice Glover deserves to be the 2013 *American Idol* winner. She had the best singing voice, the greatest range, and the best stage presence of any contestants. I'm so glad she won!

_____ No fallacy   _____ Fallacy

Name of fallacy: _____

Reason: _____

_____

6.9 Group Activities & Discussion

The Fallacy Scavenger Hunt (pp. 242-244)   (2 pages)

Here are some rules:

- Neither you nor your partner can be a "found item" on your own list.
- The only time another student can be used twice is when the student is used individually and as part of a pair.
- Any student who is to explain something must actually do it and do it correctly.

1. The definition of a fallacy found on page _____ is: _____

_____

2. A female student who can explain to you the difference between an ad hominem abusive and an *ad hominem circumstantial*.

_____

3. A male student who can explain to you the difference between an appeal to pity and an argument from compassion.

_____

4. The explanation of a false dichotomy is found on page _____.

Here is our explanation of it: _____

_____

_____

5. A student who can explain what false cause is.

_____

6. A student who can give you an example of false cause.

_____

7. A pair who can explain what hasty generalization is and give you an example of it.

_____   _____

8. A pair who can explain the difference between equivocation and amphiboly.

_____   _____

9. The explanation of appeal to force is found on page _____.

Here is our explanation of it: _____

_____

10. Two different students who can explain why critical thinkers should care about fallacies.

_____   _____

11. A pair who can explain Gladys's five suggestions for detecting and avoiding fallacies.

_____   _____

12. A student who is a Fallacy Master.

_____

13. A student who is a Fallacy Knight.

_____

14. A sticker from your teacher that shows you've found all your items.

7.1 Introduction

The "All-Time Best Ever" Thought Experiment (p. 245): What is your all-time, best ever, favorite commercial—you know—the one you actually watch? Why?

_____

_____

_____

Okay, you know this is coming—what commercial drives you crazy—you just can't turn the channel fast enough? Why?

_____

_____

_____

Student Poll (p. 246): Check all the places where you've run into advertising.

_____ Television   _____ Internet   _____ Mobile devices

_____ Video games   _____ Movies   _____ DVDs

_____ Buses   _____ Subway/BART   _____ Books

_____ Magazines   _____ Newspapers   _____ Public bathrooms

_____ Billboards   _____ Radio   _____ Other: _____

Student Poll (p. 246): On a scale from 1 ("Yes! I'm having nightmares about it!") to 10 ("No! I love those ads!"), rate how you feel about the following statement:

_____ Advertising is out of control today.

Student Poll (p. 247): Identify who you believe the top four advertisers are in the United States.

_____   _____

_____   _____

How much money in dollars do you think is spent in advertising globally? And which country do you think spends the most in advertising?

Amount spent: _____   Country: _____

7.2 The Pros and Cons of Advertising

Explaining to Aliens Thought Experiment (p. 249): Imagine that a group of aliens beamed into your house and spent a week with you. They watched television, used the internet, looked at magazines, watched the Super Bowl with you, tried out your mobile device (your choice), and even went to the mall with you. They seem to understand the culture pretty well—except for value of advertising. They just don't get it. What would you tell them? Do you think advertising has any value? If not, what would you say? If you do think advertising has value, then what? What are the benefits of it? Here's your chance to sound off.

_____

_____

_____

_____

_____

Student Poll (p. 249): On a scale from 1 ("Not happening!") to 10 ("Absolutely!"), rate the following statements.

_____ 1. Advertising encourages me to use my critical thinking skills.

_____ 2. I am easily manipulated by advertising.

_____ 3. I am able to be an independent thinker when it comes to advertising.

_____ 4. Advertising can be useful to society.

Texting and Driving Prevention PSAs Thought Experiment (pp. 251-252)

- Go to YouTube and search for: PSA commercial "On My Way." Then click on the one that says: "Glee Distracted Driving PSA: 'On My Way' (0.30)" (by U.S. Department of Transportation). Watch this 30 second PSA.

- Search for PSA commercial "5 Seconds." Then click on the one that says: "Stop the Texts. Stop the Wrecks. '5 Seconds.' PSA" (by stopthetexts). Watch this PSA.

- After you have watched both of these PSAs, which were created by the Ad Council for their campaign sponsors, then answer the questions below.

1. Who is the target audience of these PSAs? _____

2. What was the message of the PSAs?

   _____

   _____

3. How long does the average text take a driver's eyes off the road? _____

4. Was the message clear in the two PSAs? _____ Yes _____ No

5. Which PSA had the greatest impact?

   _____ "On My Way – Glee" (30 second)   _____ "5 Seconds"

6. Why did your choice of PSA have the greatest impact?

   _____

   _____

   _____

7. Do you think these PSAs would prevent your friends and classmates from texting and driving? Why or why not?

   _____

   _____

   _____

8. Would these PSAs be effective for adults 30 years old and above? Why or why not? If not, what would need to happen to make them effective?

   _____

   _____

9. Here's another PSA. This is a poster, created by Alphabetica—a New England-based graphic design collective, that was created to be a part of a campaign about preventing texting and driving. It was distributed to high schools all across the country for posting.

Do you think this would be very effective at your school or if it was posted in places where teens gather? Explain your answer.

_____

_____

_____

10. Do you think a print PSA has the same impact and effectiveness as ones you watched? Why or why not?

_____

_____

_____

My Prediction   (p. 254)

I think you'll be telling me about _____

_____

⭐ **Student Poll** (p. 255): Here are 6 criticisms of advertising. Based on your viewpoint, rank them in their order of importance, with "1" being the most important. If there is a criticism that you think is important and not listed here, then add it and rank it with the others. If there is one you don't agree with at all, then give it a zero.

_____ Advertising persuades people to buy things they don't need and/or want.

_____ Advertising reinforces harmful stereotypes.

_____ Advertising exploits children by targeting them.

_____ Advertising corrupts our culture.

_____ Advertising has inappropriate influence and control over the content of television, the news, and print magazines.

_____ Advertising manipulates consumers by using neuroscience and psychological techniques.

_____ Other: _____

"What's It Telling Me?" Thought Experiment (pp. 256-259): Study the following two ads—which are over 60 years old and typical of their time—and answer the questions.

Alcoa ad (pp. 257-258)

"Easily—without a knife blade, a bottle opener, or even a husband! All it takes is a dainty grasp, an easy two-finger twist—and the catsup is ready to pour.

We call this safe-sealing bottle cap the Alcoa HyTop. It is made of pure, food-loving Alcoa Aluminum. It spins off—and back on again—without muscle power because an exclusive Aloca process tailors it to each bottle's threads after it is on the bottle. By vacuum sealing both top and sides, the HyTop gives purity a double guard.

You'll recognize the attractive, tractable HyTop when you see it on your grocer's shelf. It's long, it's white, it's grooved—and it's on the most famous and flavorful brands. Put the bottle that wears it in your basket … save fumbling, fuming and fingers at opening time with the most cooperative cap in the world—the Alcoa HyTop Closure."

1. What product is being sold? _____

2. Who is the target audience of the ad?

_____

3. Describe the woman in the ad.

_____

_____

4. What does the copy (the words in the ad) mean?

_____

_____

5.   What does this ad tell you about how women were viewed at this time in the culture?

_____

_____

_____

6.   Do you think this ad would work today? Why or why not?

_____

_____

_____

Van Heusen ad (pp. 258-259)

For *men* only! … brand new man-talking, power-packed patterns that tell her it's a man's world …
and make her so happy it is. And man! … how that Van Heusen sewmanship makes the fine fabrics
hold their shape. And for Christmas … here's the Christmas tie that is *really* different. $2.00.

1. What product is being sold?

    _____

2. How would you describe the man in the Van Heusen ad? What does it tell you about how men were viewed in the culture at the time?

    _____

    _____

    _____

3. How would you describe the woman in the Van Heusen ad? What does it tell you about how women were viewed in the culture at the time?

    _____

    _____

    _____

4. Describe the difference in their dress and body positions.

    _____

    _____

5. Are they both equally powerful? Why or why not?

    _____

    _____

6. What does the copy (the words in the ad) mean?

    _____

    _____

7. Do you think this would be a good ad today? Why or why not?

    _____

    _____

    _____

(2 pages)

 Males in Advertising Thought Experiment (pp. 260-262): Answer the questions for each ad on the next two pages.

Dockers ad (p. 261)

1. What does this ad tell you about who men are and how they should behave?

    _____

    _____

2. What does this tell you about men and women's relationships?

    _____

    _____

3. Do you think this ad would appeal to most of the guys you know in school? Why?

    _____

    _____

Corona Extra Beer ad (pp. 261-262)

This is an ad for Corona Extra Beer. It has a target audience and a clear message about gender roles for males.

1. How would you describe the target audience?

   _____

   _____

2. What does this ad tell you about who men are and how they should behave?

   _____

   _____

⭐ **Student Poll** (p. 263): Do you think advertising can be used to fight stereotypes?

_____ Yes, I do.   _____ No way!

Have you ever seen an ad that you felt showed women as liberated and independent or men as capable of doing household chores or as caring or loving?

_____ Yes, I have.   _____ Not that I recall.

⭐ **Student Poll** (pp. 264-265): On a scale from 1 ("Horrible") to 10 ("Fantastic"), rate the following ads for how well you think they fight stereotypes.

1. AT&T/Bell Phone Co.

_____ My score

2. Ariel Laundry Soap

_____ My score

3. Noxzema (face cream)

_____ My score

4. Lego

_____ My score

⭐ **Student Poll** (p. 266): Select which number you feel reflects the spending power of children (through age 12) in the United States.

_____ $500,000,000   _____ $1,000,000,000   _____ $1,000,000,000,000

Select the number you think teenagers spend in direct sales online (called e-commerce):

_____ $100,000,000   _____ $500,000,000   _____ $1,000,000,000

💡 **"What Should a Psychologist Do?" Thought Experiment** (p. 268): Some psychologists work for companies as market researchers or consultants helping them find ways to increase the persuasive power of their advertising on children. Given what you have learned so far about advertising and children, do you think it is right for companies to use psychological theories, research, and psychologists in order to sell their products to children? Explain your answer.

_____

_____

_____

_____

_____

_____

The Who is to Blame? Thought Experiment (p. 269): This cover from *Sports Illustrated* sparked lots of discussion. Here's your turn to sound off. Answer the question posed on the cover of the magazine.

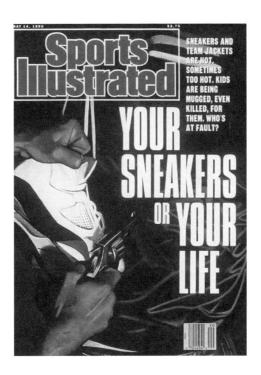

_____

_____

_____

_____

_____

_____

⭐ **Student Poll** (p. 270): On a scale from 1 ("Not at all!") to 10 ("YES!!!"), rate how you feel about the following statements.

_____ 1. Ads that use sex to sell products catch my attention.

_____ 2. Ads that use sex to sell products make me feel uncomfortable.

_____ 3. Ads should not use violence to sell their products.

⭐ **Student Poll** (p. 272): On a scale from 1 ("Not susceptible at all!") to 10 ("Super susceptible!"), rate how susceptible you think the following people or groups of people are to advertising.

_____ Myself

_____ Adults in my family

_____ My closest friends

_____ Teens in general

7.3 What Do Ads Do?

What Ads Do Quiz (p. 276):   Answer the questions based on this ad.

In this business, you've got to be decisive. So I choose milk.
Some studies suggest that teens who choose milk instead of
sugary drinks tend to be leaner, and the protein helps build
muscle. So eat right, exercise and drink 3 glasses of lowfat
or fat free milk a day. Music to my ears.

1. What product is this ad trying to inform you about? _____

2. What does this ad want you to do? _____

3. What category of ad is this? _____

4. Explain your answer to #3 and make sure you identify the direct or indirect promise that is being made.

    _____

    _____

    _____

7.4 How Ads Persuade Us: The Backstory

⭐ **Student Poll** (p. 279): On a scale from 1 ("Scandalous!") to 10 ("Brilliant"!) rate how you feel about the fact that advertisers are able to create positive brand equity without your being aware of it (let's assume that the product isn't horrible!).

_____ My score

7.5 Advertising Techniques

Transfer

 Transfer Practice I (p. 282): Answer the questions based on the Nike ad and see how well you understand transfer.

1. What does the image convey? And what feelings would be produced by it?

    _____

    _____

2. What words in the text standout? Do they make you desire anything? If so, what?

    _____

    _____

3. Taken as a whole, what does the ad associate with the brand?

    _____

    _____

4. Do you think the ad is successful? Why or why not?

    _____

    _____

    _____

Transfer Practice II (p. 283): Answer the questions about this ad that is for fabric softener sheets.

1. What images are used and what feelings might they generate?

    _____

    _____

    _____

2. What do the words in the ad, including the product name, convey? What feelings might they create
    in the consumer?

    _____

    _____

    _____

3. What feelings does the advertiser want associated with the brand?

    _____

    _____

4. How successful do you think the advertisement is in transferring positive feelings to the brand?
    Explain your answer.

    _____

    _____

Humor

(2 pages)

⭐ **Student Poll** (p. 289): On a scale from 1 ("Not funny at all!") to 10 ("Hilarious!"), rate the humorous ads and the commercial on YouTube.

1. Wiskas – "Feeding your cat's instincts"

2. Flexd Extra Tearproof Dog Leashes

3. MTV On Demand — "Hear What You Like"

4. Ameriquest Mortgage Co. — "Surprise Dinner"

Watch this ad at www.youtube.com/watch?v=gaP0aIsSINo or you can go to YouTube and search for "Surprise Dinner," Ameriquest, and select the one posted by bestcreativead—it is marked "official."

_____ 1. Wiskas — "Feeding your cat's instincts"

_____ 2. Flexd Extra Tearproof Dog Leashes

_____ 3. MTV On Demand — "Hear What You Like"

_____ 4. Ameriquest Mortgage Co. — "Surprise Dinner"

Celebrity Endorsements

⭐ **Student Poll** (p. 294): On a scale from 1 ("Never!") to 10 ("Always!"), rate how effective celebrity endorsements are.

_____ 1. Celebrity endorsements catch my attention.

_____ 2. I am willing to buy a product because a celebrity endorsed it.

Weasel Words

⭐ **Student Poll** (p. 296): On a scale from 1 ("Never!) to 10 ("Gets me every time!") rate how effective the following type of ad is in terms of getting you to stop in and shop (the actual store isn't important).

_____ My score

Use of Music

 Student Poll (p. 301): Answer the following questions about your experience shopping. If you answer "Yes" to either 1 or 2, then answer the other questions.

1. I've heard music in stores where I shop.   _____ Yes _____ No

2. I've heard music in the dressing rooms.   _____ Yes _____ No

3. The music I heard was "club-like" music.   _____ Yes _____ No

4. Listening to the music in the store makes me feel upbeat and ready to go. _____ Yes _____ No

5. The music impacted my choice to buy.   _____ Yes _____ No

Check-in (p. 302): How's it going? Rate your confidence level about how advertising works. Circle the picture that fits. No clue? Ask a friend or your teacher to coach you.

Feeling Good!

Say What?

Advertising Techniques Practice (pp. 303-314): For each ad identify the technique(s) being used.

(12 pages)

1. "David Beckham" — Instinct Sport men's fragrance

_____ Transfer

_____ Bandwagon

_____ Weasel words

_____ Humor

_____ Emotional appeal

_____ Puffery

_____ Sex

_____ Slogan, tagline

_____ Celebrity endorsement

_____ Logo

2. "Against Bad Breath." — Pedigree Dental Stix

_____ Transfer

_____ Bandwagon

_____ Weasel words

_____ Humor

_____ Emotional appeal

_____ Puffery

_____ Sex

_____ Slogan, tagline

_____ Celebrity endorsement

_____ Logo

3.   "Respect yourself in the morning." — NutriGrain

_____ Transfer

_____ Bandwagon

_____ Weasel words

_____ Humor

_____ Emotional appeal

_____ Puffery

_____ Sex

_____ Slogan, tagline

_____ Celebrity endorsement

_____ Logo

4.   "Taste the rainbow." — Skittles

_____ Transfer

_____ Bandwagon

_____ Weasel words

_____ Humor

_____ Emotional appeal

_____ Puffery

_____ Sex

_____ Slogan, tagline

_____ Celebrity endorsement

_____ Logo

5. "Find your magic at Macy's, where it all comes together." — Macy's

_____ Transfer

_____ Bandwagon

_____ Weasel words

_____ Humor

_____ Emotional appeal

_____ Puffery

_____ Sex

_____ Slogan, tagline

_____ Celebrity endorsement

_____ Logo

6. Target

_____ Transfer

_____ Bandwagon

_____ Weasel words

_____ Humor

_____ Emotional appeal

_____ Puffery

_____ Sex

_____ Slogan, tagline

_____ Celebrity endorsement

_____ Logo

7. "There's more play in a pet." — SPCA

_____ Transfer

_____ Bandwagon

_____ Weasel words

_____ Humor

_____ Emotional appeal

_____ Puffery

_____ Sex

_____ Slogan, tagline

_____ Celebrity endorsement

_____ Logo

8. "Choosy moms choose Jif." — Jif Peanut Butter

_____ Transfer

_____ Bandwagon

_____ Weasel words

_____ Humor

_____ Emotional appeal

_____ Puffery

_____ Sex

_____ Slogan, tagline

_____ Celebrity endorsement

_____ Logo

9. "Marilyn Monroe discovers the world's most glamorous make-up.
    Acclaimed by Hollywood" — Jon-Joy cosmetics

_____ Transfer

_____ Bandwagon

_____ Weasel words

_____ Humor

_____ Emotional appeal

_____ Puffery

_____ Sex

_____ Slogan, tagline

_____ Celebrity endorsement

_____ Logo

10. "True Divers Don't Need Water." — Nike Fütbol

_____ Transfer

_____ Bandwagon

_____ Weasel words

_____ Humor

_____ Emotional appeal

_____ Puffery

_____ Sex

_____ Slogan, tagline

_____ Celebrity endorsement

_____ Logo

11. "There's a much juicier chew." — Juicy Fruit Gum

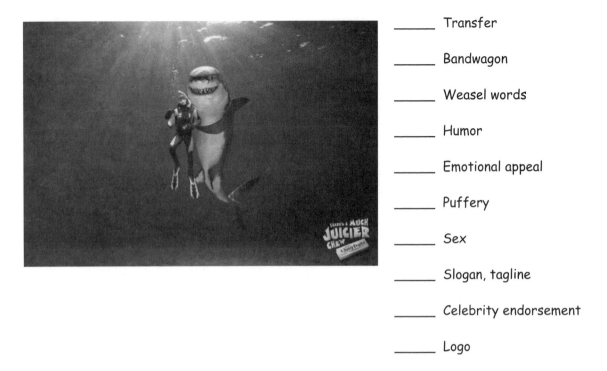

_____ Transfer

_____ Bandwagon

_____ Weasel words

_____ Humor

_____ Emotional appeal

_____ Puffery

_____ Sex

_____ Slogan, tagline

_____ Celebrity endorsement

_____ Logo

12. "We Put the Protein in the pro.
     Packed with 100% lean meat and healthy veggies. Fill Up On The Good Stuff." — Campbell's Soup

_____ Transfer

_____ Bandwagon

_____ Weasel words

_____ Humor

_____ Emotional appeal

_____ Puffery

_____ Sex

_____ Slogan, tagline

_____ Celebrity endorsement

_____ Logo

Answer the following questions about these ads:

13. "Become a Hero. (p. 309)
     Help homeless dogs every time you redeem a Hero Coupon
     Here's How: Save $15 with the Hero Coupons found inside
     specially marked bags of PEDIGREE® Food for Dogs
     You're the Hero. For every Hero Coupon redeemed
     PEDIGREE will match the value with a donation to PetSmart Charities.
     Really good food for dogs. Dogsrule.com" — PEDIGREE Dog Food

a. What do you have to do to become a Hero?

     _____

     _____

b. What is required to redeem a coupon?

     _____

     _____

c. When you become a hero who is benefited? Mark the ones that apply.

     _____ Homeless dogs   _____ Pedigree   _____ Me

d. This is a _____ good ad   _____ bad ad because:

     _____

     _____

14. Campbell's soup (pp. 310-311)

A man likes to share good things with people he likes. And soup's one of them. Good things happen when you have soup. It makes you feel good. It tastes good. Coaxes appetites along and lest you enjoy the rest of the meal.

And soup is so right for a man of any age — gives him the kind of good eating he likes. Good meat broths and meats, nourishing vegetables, dairy products, cereals. No nonsense about soup. You get proteins, minerals and vitamins in every spoonful.

Every man has his favorite soup. These two have chosen Campbell's Vegetable. There are 15 different vegetables in this soup (just for fun, count them up — they're listed on the label), gently seasoned and simmered in meat broth. Can you blame them for making it their favorite?

Have some yourself and see what good things begin to happen. You can have soup ready in just 4 minutes ... to warm you up ... to gentle you down ... to make you feel good all over. **Say** ... have you had your soup today?

a. How does the image of the boy and dad eating their soup together make you feel? Why?

_____

_____

b. What are the dominant colors in this ad?

_____

c. Why do you think these colors were chosen?

_____

_____

d. How many times does the word "good" appear in this ad? _____

e. Why do you think they use the word "good" so many times?

_____

_____

f. In the copy we are told three times that good things begin to happen when people eat soup. What are some of the good things that happen according to the copy?

_____

_____

g. How does this copy make you feel: "… to warm you up … to gentle you down … to make you feel good all over"?

_____

_____

h. Does this ad make you want to try Campbell's soup? _____ Why?

_____

_____

i. On a scale from 1 ("Loser!") to 10 ("I'm dreaming of soup!"), rate how effective you think this ad is.

_____ My rating

15. "The Mini automatic. For simple driving." — Mini (1971 Clubman Automatic) (pp. 312-313)

The Mini automatic does one little thing more for you.

It changes gear without you changing gear. This little thing can make a world of difference in all kinds of driving conditions.

In congested traffic you don't fight a running battle with the gear stick. The gearbox fights its own battles.

When you're driving fast you keep both hands on the wheel all the time, which makes for a safer ride. And whenever you feel like a bit of fast armwork through the bends, you can switch from automatic to manual.

Then our automatic has some hidden benefits. You can't stall on the clutch because there's no clutch pedal to stall on.

You can't grind into the wrong gear because you don't change gear. In fact the Mini automatic is the closest thing you'll find to a built-in chauffeur.

It makes driving as effortless as sleeping. Sleeping, luv. You lie down, close your eyes and …

Mini: greatest invention since the wheel.

a. Based on the expression on the woman's face, what do you think she is feeling?

_____

b. What do you think the ad is trying to say based on the picture and the copy "The Mini automatic. For simple driving" found on the image?

_____

_____

c. Read the rest of the copy in the ad. What is your takeaway about driving the Mini automatic?

_____

_____

d. The woman in the ad is a look-alike of Goldie Hawn, an Academy Award winning actress, who was very popular at the time of the ad. In fact, Goldie Hawn had been a part of the popular TV show "Laugh-in" around this time and played a ditzy blonde who had a high-pitched laugh and the same type of expression on her face that the look-alike has. How would this affect how people in 1971 would understand this ad in terms of women drivers?

_____

_____

_____

e. Do you think this ad would work well today? Why?

_____

_____

_____

f. On a scale from 1 ("Lousy!") to 10 ("Spot on!"), rate how effective you think this ad is.

_____ My rating

16. "Guy + more guys + 'Ja, but how do you know that it hurts' = (image of the three guys who are about to touch an electrified fence). That's why we insure women." — First for Women Insurance Company Limited. (p. 314)

a. Based on this ad, why does the insurance company only cover women?

_____

b. Do you think that is why they really only insure women? _____

c. Why do you think they produced this ad with this image and copy?

_____

_____

d. Does this ad catch your attention? _____

e. Would you remember the company based on the ad? _____

f. Do you like this ad? _____ Explain why:

_____

_____

7.6 Regulating Advertising

⭐ **Student Poll** (p. 316): On a scale from 1 ("No, I don't agree!") to 10 ("Yes, I agree."), rate the following statements.

_____ 1. Photoshopping of images in advertising is okay to do.

_____ 2. Photoshopping creates a false reality of what male and female models and celebrities really look like.

_____ 3. My self-image and self-esteem are affected by the images I see in advertising and other media.

7.8 "Cool Hunting"

⭐ **Student Poll** (p. 321): On a scale from 1 ("Not true!") to 10 ("Absolutely!"), rate the following statements.

_____   1. I "Like" things because I want people to know who I am.

_____   2. You are what you "Like."

_____   3. I don't mind if my "Likes" are free advertising for companies.

_____   4. The more "Likes" or "followers" I get, the better!

⭐ **Student Poll** (p. 322): Indicate whether you "Agree" or "Disagree" with the following statements.

_____   1. I like when brands, such as Doritos, have me send in videos or selfies.

_____   2. Companies are not "using me" if they have contests or promotions that I can participate in.

⭐ **Student Poll** (p. 322): Answer the following questions.

1.   I have seen ads appear on the webpages I visit that relate to what I like and the kinds of items I buy.

   _____ Yes _____ No

2.   I like targeted advertising.   _____ Yes _____ No

⭐ **Student Poll** (p. 323): On as scale from 1 ("Not true at all!") to 10 ("Absolutely true!"), rate the following statements.

_____   1. It is okay for advertisers and corporations to use any technique that works with the teen market.

_____   2. I don't feel manipulated by advertisers when I "Like" a brand.

_____   3. Teens need to own that they make the decisions for their purchases.

Important Takeaways

Three important takeaways that I want to remember from this chapter are:

1. _____

_____

_____

2. _____

_____

_____

3. _____

_____

_____

7.10 Individual Activities

1. **Needs vs. Wants** (p. 328): Part of being a good critical thinker when it comes to advertising is to understand the difference between your needs and wants. The problem for all of us is that sometimes we mix up the two—and advertising encourages that!

   Has there ever been a time when you found something in the store that you hadn't gone in to buy and you felt you just HAD to have it?

   _____ Yes   _____ No

   If you answered yes, did you feel you NEEDED to have it?

   _____ Yes   _____ No

   As you think about it now, did you *really* need it at the time?

   _____ Yes   _____ No

   List five things you're planning to buy or expect to buy soon and the cost (if you're not sure of the exact cost, then estimate). Leave the other two boxes empty.

Item	Cost	Need	Want

   - Are these items things that you need to use every day, such as food for lunch, sports equipment, grooming products, items for school, or a hobby?

   - If you plan to buy clothes, then do you need to have them or would it be nice to have them?

   - Are these items things that would be fun to have but that you could live without?

   Based on these questions, mark whether the items are a need or a want.

   It's okay to want something, but know whether what you are buying is a need or a want. This can help you manage your spending and not get swept away by ads.

2. **Viewing Ads as a Critical Thinker** (pp. 329-330): For each ad, answer the following questions.

Mountain Dew ad (p. 329): DON'T BE FOOLED BY A NAME: Diet Dew™ has everything you love about regular Dew,™ without the calories. And now it's got a great new taste. HOW DEW DOES DIET.

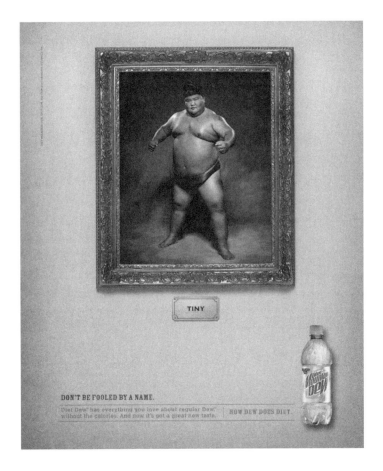

1. What is the message? _____

_____

2. Who is the target audience? _____

3. What persuasive techniques are used? _____

_____

4. Is this ad successful? Why or why not? _____

_____

_____

Impaired Driving Ad (p. 330)

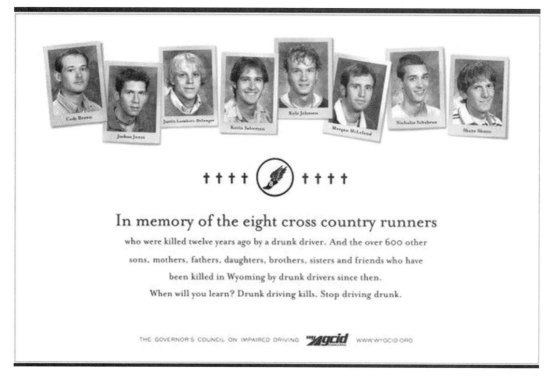

In memory of the eight cross country runners
who were killed twelve years ago by a drunk driver. And the over 600 other
sons, mothers, fathers, daughters, brothers, sisters and friends who have
been killed in Wyoming by drunk drivers since then.
When will you learn? Drunk driving kills. Stop driving drunk.

1. What is the message? _____

   _____

2. How do the images and text work together to create the message?

   _____

   _____

3. Who is the target audience? _____

4. What persuasive techniques are used? _____

   _____

5. Is this ad successful? Why or why not? _____

   _____

   _____

3. **Does Advertising determine your tastes?** (p. 331)

The American Association of Advertising Agencies created a full-page ad regarding the impact of advertising on us. The ad shows a middle-aged woman sitting in a chair wearing the same style of clothing, hat, and hairstyle as the woman on the television and even sitting in the same manner. The ad states clearly that advertising does not determine what people like; rather, advertising is a mirror of society's likes. In fact, they emphasize that advertising "is another word for freedom of choice." They claim that advertising doesn't determine what we like or want because we have a mind of our own and only buy what we want—that advertising is really only a response to what people want.

In your opinion, is the American Association of Advertising Agencies correct that advertising does not shape what we like and buy? Is advertising really only a response to what people want? Explain your answer.

_____

_____

_____

_____

_____

_____

_____

_____

_____

_____

⭐ **Student Poll** (p. 331): On a scale from 1 ("Nobody influences me!") to 10 ("My mind has been taken over!"), rate the following statement.

_____ Advertising influences my desires, wants, and choices.

4. **Whatever Works** (p. 332)

You are with some friends and one of them—Julie—shows the group an ad for Relish clothing. It shows two beautiful, thin, fashionably dressed women being arrested. One officer is yanking the scarf around the neck of one of the women and pulling her neck back while she appears handcuffed. The other woman, wearing a very short dress, is pushed by another officer over the hood of the car while he runs his hand up the bottom of her dress. The women do not appear to be enjoying what is happening to them. The copy at the bottom says "Relish it."

Some of your friends are very upset with the ad saying this objectifies and dehumanizes women as well as supports violence against women. However, Steve—one of your other friends—strongly disagrees saying that the ad does what it is supposed to do—which is to get you to notice it and remember it—that sensational and shocking ads sell more products than ads that aren't shocking. Then Julie turns to you and asks you what you think about the ad. What do you say?

_____

_____

_____

_____

_____

_____

_____

_____

_____

_____

⭐ **Student Poll** (p. 332): On a scale from 1 ("Very strict limits!") to 10 ("Absolutely no limits!"), rate the following statement.

_____   Advertising should have no limits placed on it in terms of what is shocking and sensational—after all, that is what gets ads noticed and remembered.

5. **Billboard Ad** (p. 333): This is your billboard to design. Everyday thousands of people will see it. What do you think is important to say to them?

7.11 Group Activities & Discussion

2. **To Photoshop or Not?** (p. 334)

In small groups have the students discuss the following scenario: They work at an advertising agency that advertises a particular fashion brand to the teen market. Your boss wants your team to make recommendations regarding whether or not to use any real-sized models and about Photoshopping the models.

You are all well aware of what went on at *Seventeen* magazine and *Vogue* over teenage girls being upset about these magazines using only very thin models and then even Photoshopping the models. Currently, you use teen size 1 or 3. Discuss whether or not you should include more real-sized girls in your ads, and make sure you talk about both the pros and cons of using real-sized girls. Also, you use Photoshop extensively to make the clothes look better on the models and to make the faces of the models prettier (such as to erase acne). The advertisers are quite pleased with the results when you use thin models and use Photoshop. Should you continue doing this? What are the pros and cons?

Finally, what are your recommendations to your boss?

Our recommendation regarding the use of real-sized models is:

_____

Our recommendation(s) regarding the Photoshopping of models is/are :

_____

_____

8.1 Introduction

⭐ **Student Poll** (p. 337): On a scale from 1 ("Not important!") to 10 ("Super important!"), rate the importance of understanding direct and circumstantial evidence, particularly eyewitness testimony, for critical thinkers.

I rate the importance as a _____.

Here's why: _____

_____

_____

My Prediction (p. 338)

I think you'll being telling me about _____

_____

8.2 What Is Direct Evidence?

⭐ **The Direct Evidence Student Poll** (p. 339): Check the items that you think are examples of direct evidence.

_____ Eyewitness testimony	_____ Fingerprints
_____ Hearsay	_____ Motive
_____ Confessions	_____ Surveillance tapes
_____ Ownership of the murder weapon	_____ Receipts
_____ Physical evidence of a crime	_____ DNA

8.3 What Is Circumstantial Evidence

The "Which Is Which?" Quiz (p. 340): Identify which type of evidence is demonstrated below and why.

1. A witness says that she saw it raining on the night of the murder.

    This is an example of _____ evidence because _____

    _____

2. A witness says that she saw a man come into the diner on the night of the murder and he was wearing a raincoat covered in water drops, so it must have been raining.

    This is an example of _____ evidence because _____

    _____

8.4 A Closer Look

⭐ **Student Poll** (p. 341): Check which statement you think is the most accurate in regards to direct evidence and circumstantial evidence.

_____ Only direct evidence can be used to establish the guilt of the defendant.

_____ Only circumstantial evidence can be used to establish the guilt of the defendant.

_____ Either one can be used to establish the guilt of the defendant.

_____ In order to establish the guilt of the defendant, both kinds of evidence must be used.

(3 pages)

 Evidence and Inference Practice (pp. 342-344): Analyze the facts and evidence. Identify the type of evidence for each piece of evidence. Also state and explain the inferences you are able to draw based on these facts and evidence.

Case Notes: On August 30, 2013, the body of Charlie Wise was found 100 yards off of a public access road in a remote wooded area. A red handkerchief was used as a gag, and he had a contact gunshot wound to his head. The bullet recovered from the head was from a .40 Smith and Wesson gun. The coroner determined that Wise had died from a gunshot wound to the head and that due to the decomposition of the body, the time of death was near to the time of his disappearance on July 15, 2013. Two men, Phillip Maze and Terrance Robinson, were arrested for the kidnapping and murder of Charlie Wise.

1. Facts: Two witnesses, Sarah Leigh and Harry Hodges, saw two men angrily confront Wise, shouting and pushing him, before the abduction in the late afternoon in a parking lot. Neither of the witnesses knew the two men, though both knew Wise. Each witness described the shorter man as wearing a black tee shirt with the Seattle Seahawks logo on it, jeans, and a black baseball cap; and the taller man as wearing a navy pullover hoodie and jeans with a red handkerchief sticking out of the back pants pocket. Both witnesses saw the men wearing black gloves, and both remarked that it seemed odd on a hot summer afternoon. Leigh also saw the shorter man pull out a gun, fire it twice in the air, and force Wise into the trunk of a blue 1985 Oldsmobile, and the taller man shut the trunk. Both men got into the car, with the shorter man driving, and the car sped off. Leigh immediately called the police. Two spent shell casings recovered at the scene of the abduction were from a .40 Smith and Wesson gun.

Identify the types of evidence provided in the Case Notes and in the Facts:

_____

_____

_____

_____

The inferences I can draw:

_____

_____

_____

_____

2. Facts: At 9:15 p.m. on the day of the kidnapping the police stopped a blue 1985 Oldsmobile driven by a man named Philip Maze for speeding. He was wearing a black tee shirt with the Seattle Seahawks logo on it, jeans, and a black baseball cap. On the front seat was a pair of black gloves with gunshot residue on them. There was some blood splatter and gun residue on the shirt Maze was wearing. The blood was tested and found to match the blood type of the victim, which was AB+, a blood type that only 3% of the U.S. population has. A strand of hair that matches that of the victim was found in the trunk of the Oldsmobile Maze was driving.

The types of evidence provided:

_____

_____

_____

The inferences I can draw:

_____

_____

_____

3. Facts: A .40 Smith and Wesson gun was found hidden in Maze's garage in a box of Christmas decorations. The coroner removed a .40 Smith and Wesson bullet from the victim's head. The Ballistics Laboratory matched this bullet to the gun found in Maze's garage, which was registered to him. The Ballistics Laboratory also matched the two spent shell casings recovered at the site of the abduction to his gun.

The types of evidence provided:

_____

_____

_____

The inferences I can draw:

_____

_____

_____

4. Final facts: Robinson signed a statement confessing that only Maze had a gun, Maze alone held the gun, and that Maze shot Wise. Robinson admitted that the red handkerchief, which belonged to him, was used for a gag and that he was the one to gag the victim when they kidnapped him, but he did not want Wise killed.

The crime was committed in a state where if a murder is committed during a felony crime, then all the defendants involved in the crime are considered equally responsible for the murder whether or not they wished or planned for someone to die. Kidnapping is a felony crime.

Based on all the facts presented, if you were on the jury what conclusions would you draw about the innocence or guilt of Maze and Robinson?

Phillip Maze:

    Kidnapping   Innocent _____   Guilty _____

    Murder   Innocent _____   Guilty _____

Terrance Robinson:

    Kidnapping   Innocent _____   Guilty _____

    Murder   Innocent _____   Guilty _____

Explain the reasoning behind your conclusions:

_____

_____

_____

_____

_____

_____

Do you need to revise your prediction? If so, do it here. (p. 344)

_____

_____

The Evidence Quiz (pp. 345-346): Read each scenario below and answer the questions.

1. Mr. Thomas is on trial for murdering Mr. Simms by shooting him. You are part of a jury deliberating over whether it is reasonable to conclude that Mr. Thomas murdered Mr. Simms. Based on the testimony and any other information provided, what verdict would you vote for and why. Make sure you identify the type of evidence presented in the case.

A witness testified that shortly after she came into the store to pay for her gas, she saw Mr. Thomas enter the store covered in blood and carrying a gun. He came in immediately after she heard gunfire outside the store where Mr. Simms was found dead. The forensic scientist verified that the blood on Mr. Thomas belonged to Mr. Simms, the bullet recovered from the body came from the gun Mr. Thomas was carrying, and there was gunshot residue on Mr. Thomas's hand.

Based on the evidence, I conclude that Mr. Thomas is _____ innocent _____ guilty

of the crime because _____

_____

_____

_____

_____

2. Jake Winston is on trial for assaulting and robbing Mrs. Ames in the parking lot of Lotsa Stuff. You are on a jury that is ready to vote on the verdict. Based on the testimony and any other information provided, what verdict would you vote for? Why? Make sure you identify the type of evidence presented in the case.

Mrs. Ames testified that she had left Lotsa Stuff and was on her way to her car when a white man in his early twenties in a grey hoodie and jeans approached her asking for money for gas. She told him he that she did not have any cash as she had spent it in the store. She said the

defendant got angry and knocked her to the ground, grabbed her purse, and ran. She screamed for help, and a teenage boy named John Willard ran over to help her up. He then called the police. The police took a description of the man who had assaulted and robbed her. They found a white man in his early twenties wearing a grey hoodie and jeans running a block from the store. They took him in for questioning and to be a part of a lineup. He did not have a purse, and he did not have any money on him. His identification said his name was Jake Winston. Mrs. Ames identified him in a lineup as the man who knocked her down and stole her purse. John Willard also identified him in a lineup as the man he saw knock Mrs. Ames down and run off with the purse.

Based on the evidence, I conclude that Jake Winston is _____ innocent _____ guilty

of the crime because _____

_____

_____

_____

_____

 Check-in (p. 346):   Rate your confidence level for understanding direct and circumstantial evidence and drawing inferences. Write a caption for the picture that fits. No clue? Ask a friend or teacher to coach you.

_____   _____

8.5 Eyewitness Testimony and Memory

The Power of Eyewitness Testimony Thought Experiment (p. 347): Why do you think that a jury is more affected by eyewitness testimony than any other type of evidence? Do you think that's the way it should be? Why or why not?

_____

_____

_____

_____

⭐ **Student Poll** (p. 348): State your agreement or disagreement with the following statements by writing "Yes" or "No." No sitting on the fence! Which way do you lean? "Yes" or "No"?

_____ 1. My memory is like a video recorder, recording everything that happens.

_____ 2. My memory does not record everything that happens.

_____ 3. My memory is permanent.

_____ 4. My memory isn't permanent.

_____ 5. My memory records everything precisely as it happens.

_____ 6. My memory changes—some of my old memories fade away.

The Selective Attention Thought Experiment (p. 350): Go to the URL listed and then click on the link and watch the video clip: http://viscog.beckman.illinois.edu/flashmovie/15.php, or go to www.criticalthinking.com/practicalct and click on the link for this activity.

Note: You should end up at the Visual Cognition Lab at the University of Illinois. If you have problems, then search for Visual Cognition Lab University of Illinois and then select the result with the URL for this activity.

This is a visual perception test that focuses on "selective attention." It is a video that is often used in industrial safety training. Follow the directions and see how well you do. Your participation in this experiment will help make what we are going to talk about meaningful and relevant.

In the video there are two teams, one wearing white and the other black. Count the number of times the team wearing white passes the basketball.

The team wearing white passed the basketball _____ times.

The correct answer is _____.

What did you learn from watching this video? _____

_____

_____

_____

⭐ **Student Poll** (p. 350): Write "Yes" or "No" for each statement.

_____ 1. I notice when things change around me.

_____ 2. I notice unexpected things when they happen.

_____ 3. When something important happens, I am aware, taking in all the details.

The *Change Blindness* Thought Experiment 1 (p. 351): Go to the URL listed and watch "NOVA/Inside NOVA: Change Blindness." http://www.youtube.com/watch?v=VkrrVozZR2c, or go to www.criticalthinking.com/practicalct and click on the link for this activity.

You can also find it by searching the title on YouTube. It is posted by NOVA PBS.

At the beginning of the video you will be involved in an experiment.

How did you do? _____

Match the term with its definition:

1. _____ Inattentional blindness   2. _____ Change blindness

a. "The failure to notice something that is fully obvious right there in front of you when your attention is engaged on something or someone else."

b. "The failure to notice a difference between what's there right now and what was there a moment ago."

In the experiment of the man asking directions, 50% of the people failed to notice the switch in men. Dr. Simons explains why this happens. If you need to, listen to his explanation again, and then explain why this happens in your own words.

_____

_____

_____

Dr. Simons explains that the goal of seeing is not to build a complete photograph in your mind but to make sense of the meaning of the world around you. Select either true or false.

_____ True   _____ False

The Change Blindness Thought Experiment 2 (p. 352): Go to the URL listed and watch "Experimental Psychology – Change Blindness" posted by Fabrizio Bonacci.
http://youtube.com/watch?v=38XO7ac9eSs, or go to www.criticalthinking.com/practicalct and click on the link for this activity.

You can also find it by searching the title on YouTube. It is posted by Fabrizio Bonacci.

What unusual thing happened after the people signed the consent form?

_____

_____

What percent of people did not notice any change? _____

What did you learn from watching this video? _____

_____

_____

_____

8.6 The Reliability of Eyewitness Testimony

The Eyewitness Testimony Thought Experiment (p. 353): You are an expert on memory and perception who has been called to testify in court about whether or not eyewitness testimony is always reliable. Based on what you've learned already, what would you say?

_____

_____

_____

_____

_____

_____

(2 pages)

 The "Getting It Right" Thought Experiment (pp. 356-357): Go to the following URL and watch the video: "Eyewitness Identification – Getting it Right."

http://www.innocenceproject.org/causes-wrongful-conviction/eyewitness-misidentification, or go to www.criticalthinking.com/practicalct and click on the link for this activity. Then answer the following questions.

Jennifer Thompson   Ronald Cotton

1. Why did Jennifer Thompson feel that she would be able to identify her assailant?

_____

_____

_____

2. At the photographic lineup, what did Jennifer feel her job was?

_____

3. While Jennifer said she was certain of her identification, did she do anything that might suggest that she really wasn't certain? Explain your answer.

_____

_____

4. Did anything happen after the lineup to boost Jennifer's confidence about her identification? Explain your answer.

_____

_____

Images used with permission from the Innonence Project.

5. The video talks about laboratory studies where the researchers compare groups of participants who receive positive feedback after their identifications to a control group who did not receive feedback. What did these studies show?

_____

_____

6. Ronald Cotton was the only man in the lineup whose picture had been in the photographic lineup. What effect, if any, would this have on Jennifer's identification of him in the live lineup?

_____

_____

7. Did anything happen after the live lineup to further boost Jennifer's confidence about her identification? How certain was she at the trial? Explain your answer.

_____

_____

_____

8. How many years did Ronald Cotton spend in prison before he was exonerated of the crime? What was used to exonerate him?

_____

9. If you were in charge of deciding what evidence would be allowed to be used in your state, would you allow eyewitness testimony as evidence? Why or why not?

_____

_____

_____

_____

_____

_____

Solutions for Making Eyewitness Testimony More Reliable

⭐ **Student Poll** (p. 358): On a scale from 1 ("Totally unreliable!") to 10 ("Super reliable!"), rate how reliable these solutions will make eyewitness identification.

_____ My rating on the reliability of these solutions.

Important Takeaways

Three important takeaways that I want to remember from this chapter are:

1. _____

   _____

   _____

2. _____

   _____

   _____

3. _____

   _____

   _____

8.8 Individual Activities

1. **Recall Challenge** (pp. 362 and 364): You will need to have someone time you, set a timer, or use a stopwatch. View the pictures on page 364 for 1 minute. You may not write anything down. Then turn back to this page and write down as many of the pictures as you can remember.

_____   _____

_____   _____

_____   _____

_____   _____

_____   _____

_____   _____

_____   _____

_____   _____

_____   _____

2. **Perception Test I** (p. 363): Are these lines different sizes or the same size?

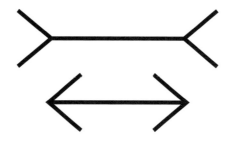

These lines are: _____

3. **Perception Test II** (p. 363): Check all the color palettes that are the same.

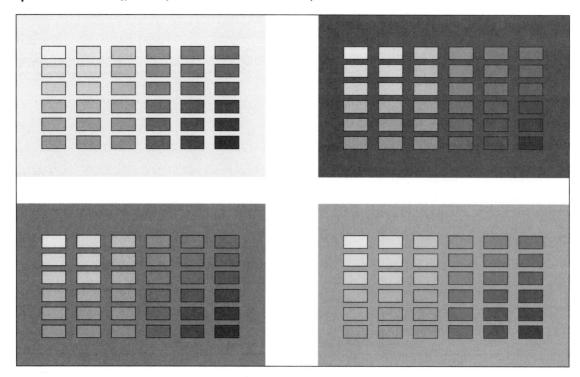

a. _____ The palette in the yellow box

b. _____ The palette in the blue box

c. _____ The palette in the pink box

d. _____ The palette in the green box

e. _____ None of the palettes

Activity 1: Recall Challenge: You have one minute to memorize all 20 items. When you are done, return to page 362 and write down as many of the pictures as you can remember.

4. **The Crime Scene** (p. 365): The lead detective has discovered a problem with the crime scene photos. Someone has tampered with the crime scene. See how many differences you can spot between the two photographs of the same crime scene.

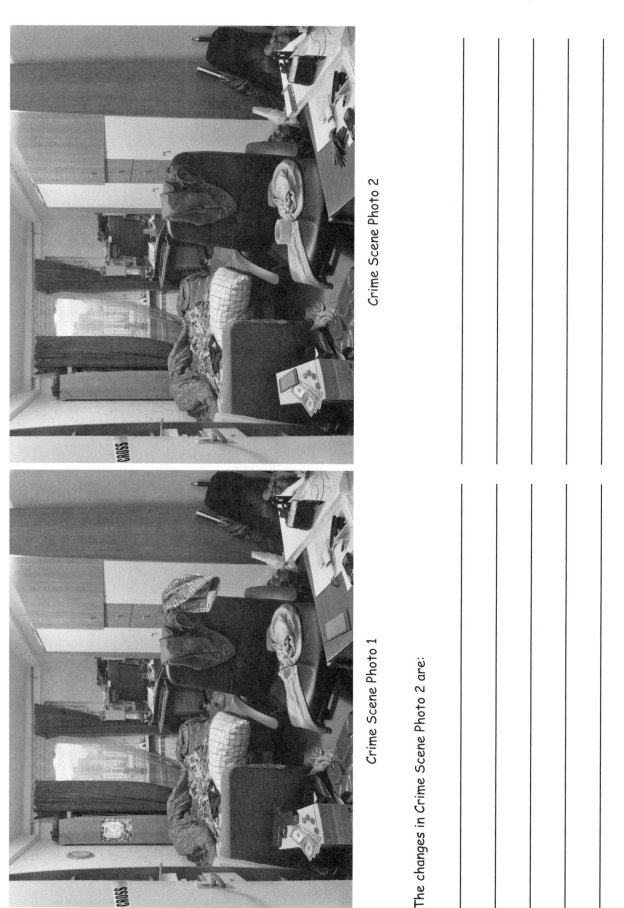

Crime Scene Photo 2

Crime Scene Photo 1

The changes in Crime Scene Photo 2 are:

8.9 Group Activities & Discussion

(6 pages)

The Case of the Murder of Robert Head (pp. 366-371)
Divide into small groups of 4 students who will be members of a jury. Have them work through this case. They need to discuss the questions and come to a decision as a group, including their rationale.

The Crime: On April 1, sometime during the early morning hours, Robert Head was beaten and stabbed 14 times by an unknown assailant. He died in the hospital as a result of the stabbings and injuries that resulted from the beating. He was never able to give a statement to police.

The Investigation (p. 366): Police found four eyewitnesses. Three people told police they witnessed the fight that occurred between Robert Head and the assailant. The fourth witness claimed to have seen a man hiding from police who had blood on his hand. All four witnesses identified Maurice Patterson in a live lineup. A bloody knife was found near the scene.

Based on this information, do you think Maurice Patterson committed the murder? Have a vote and record the numbers. Then poll the jury as to why. Record the reasons below.

_____ Yes   _____ No   _____ Undecided

"Yes" reasons: _____

_____

_____

"No" reasons: _____

_____

_____

"Undecided" reasons: _____

_____

_____

The Eyewitness Testimony (p. 367): The three people who witnessed the fight had only a fleeting glimpse of the fight and only in the dark. All four witnesses identified Maurice Patterson in the live lineup weeks after the attack. They, also, only testified regarding these identifications after being threatened with contempt of court (not obeying an order of the court—which can lead to fines and/or jail time).

Based on this additional information, do you think Maurice Patterson committed the murder? Record the number of votes for each answer. If anyone on the jury has changed his or her answer, then record the reason why.

_____ Yes _____ No _____ Undecided

Reasons for changing vote to "Yes":

_____

_____

Reasons for changing vote to "No":

_____

_____

Reasons for changing vote to "Undecided":

_____

_____

The DNA Evidence (pp. 367-368):   The bloody knife was sent to Orchid Cellmark for DNA testing. The DNA testing looks at the autosomal DNA, which is DNA present on 22 of the 23 pairs of chromosomes of each individual. Specifically, in criminal cases the interest is in the autosomal STR (Short Tandem Repeats) DNA. 99.9% of all DNA in humans is the same for everyone; however, 0.1% is different. This is what is examined in routine autosomal STR testing because it is highly variable from one person to the next. The STR test results excluded Patterson, indicating a mixture of the victim's profile and an unknown profile. When the unknown profile was compared to the State CODIS (The Combined DNA Index System managed by the FBI), it was found that the unknown profile belonged to a drug addict who had a violent history. The Cook County State's Attorney's Office, however, was never directly notified by the Police Forensic Science Center that the sample included the victim's blood. This oversight would have presumably led the prosecutors to believe that the knife was unrelated the Robert Head's murder. As a result, the prosecutors continued with the case against Maurice Patterson.

Based on this additional information, do you think Maurice Patterson committed the murder? Record the number of votes for each answer. If anyone on the jury has changed his or her answer, then record the reason why.

_____ Yes   _____ No   _____ Undecided

Reasons for changing vote to "Yes":

_____

_____

Reasons for changing vote to "No":

_____

_____

Reasons for changing vote to "Undecided":

_____

_____

The Trial—the Alibi (p. 368): Maurice Patterson's alibi was that he was at home with his wife and stepdaughters when the murder occurred. Patterson's trial counsel did not call any of the family to testify about whether or not he was at home as he claimed.

As a jury does it make a difference to you whether or not his family testified in regards to his alibi? Why?

Number of jury: _____ Yes   _____ No

Why "Yes":

_____

_____

Why "No":

_____

_____

The Trial—Other Defense Testimony (p. 369): Maurice Patterson's trial counsel did not present any witnesses and did not permit Patterson to testify even though he maintained his innocence throughout the trial.

As a jury does it make a difference to you whether or not Maurice Patterson testified? Why?

Number of jury: _____ Yes   _____ No

Why "Yes":

_____

_____

Why "No":

_____

_____

The Trial—the Prosecution (p. 369): The prosecution argued that because the victim's DNA was not found on the knife (remember, the prosecution was never directly notified that the sample from the knife included the victim's blood), it was not the murder weapon, so it was possible that Patterson was the perpetrator. Their case rested solely on the eyewitness testimony and the identification of Maurice Patterson in the live lineup.

Based on all of the information you know, do you think Maurice Patterson committed the murder? Have a vote and record the numbers. Then poll the jury as to why. These reasons will help in the jury's interview with CNN.

_____ Yes   _____ No   _____ Undecided

CNN Jury Interview (p. 369)

In an interview after the trial, the jury will be asked by CNN about the reasoning behind their decision. How will you as a jury answer?

_____

_____

_____

_____

 **The Actual Verdict**[8] (p. 370): On November 19, 2003, Maurice Patterson was convicted by a jury of first-degree murder and sentenced to 20 years in prison. While in prison, Patterson filed a Freedom of Information request to obtain the lab report on the knife. His appellate attorneys were informed in 2008 that the victim's blood had been found on the knife. This disproved the prosecution's main argument and confirmed that the knife, found near the crime scene, was indeed the murder weapon. Based on this information, the judge ordered a new trial in November 2009. Patterson remained an additional 11 months behind bars waiting for the trial. On October 8, 2010, with the help of the Center on Wrongful Convictions, prosecutors dropped all charges against Maurice Patterson and he was released from prison. He served seven years in prison for a crime he did not commit.

Record your personal response as a jury member to this question: What do you think of the actual verdict?

_____

_____

_____

_____

As a group discuss the following:

1. What did you think of the actual verdict?

2. What could the criminal justice system do to prevent other people from spending time in prison for a crime they did not commit? Record your group's ideas below.

_____

_____

_____

_____

_____

_____

8. The Innocence Project. Photo used with permission.

The Jury and Critical Thinking (p. 371): Discuss as a jury what importance, if any, critical thinking plays for jury members. Summarize your conclusions here to present to the class.

_____

_____

_____

_____

_____

_____

Large Group Discussion (p. 371): Discuss the following questions.

1.   What evidence was critical to this case? Why?

2.   Did your votes as a jury change as you received more information about the case? Why?

3.   What safeguards could have been put in place to see that a wrongful conviction did not occur?

4.   What importance, if any, does critical thinking play in serving on a jury?